More Money Than Month

To Rick —
Let's spend a make
lots of money together!
All the best! Thanks
for everything

All Rights Reserved
© MMVIII by Todd Dean

This book may not be reproduced in whole or in part, by any means, without written consent of the publisher.

LIFE SUCCESS PUBLISHING, LLC
8900 E Pinnacle Peak Road, Suite D240
Scottsdale, AZ 85255

Telephone: 800.473.7134
Fax: 480.661.1014
E-mail: admin@lifesuccesspublishing.com

ISBN (hardcover) 978-1-59930-256-0
ISBN (ebook)   978-1-59930-257-7

Cover :   Lloyd Arbour & LifeSuccess Publishing, LLC
Text: Lloyd Arbour & LifeSuccess Publishing, LLC
Edit: Publication Services Inc.

COMPANIES, ORGANIZATIONS, INSTITUTIONS, AND INDUSTRY PUBLICATIONS: Quantity discounts are available on bulk purchases of this book for reselling, educational purposes, subscription incentives, gifts, sponsorship, or fundraising. Special books or book excerpts can also be created to fit specific needs such as private labeling with your logo on the cover and a message from a VIP printed inside. For more information, please contact our Special Sales Department at LifeSuccess Publishing, LLC.

More Money Than Month

Stop Stressing Over Your Finances and Take Control of Your Life

Todd Dean

Foreword by Bob Proctor

Acknowledgements and Dedications

I would like to thank Dee Burks and Liz Ragland and the entire team at TAG Media Solutions for their tireless work and effort, and for their putting up with my endless phone calls and emails. Without you, this book would not have been possible!

To Bob Proctor and Gerry Robert, who helped guide me to the vision that this book has become, and for their ongoing support and guidance. I can't thank you enough.

To Charles, Alina, and all of the other people who were featured in the book, I thank you from the bottom of my heart. Without your stories, this book would have been without that human element that every story needs at its core. I thank you for your honesty and support.

To the team at LifeSuccess Publishing, I thank you for your insight, direction, and occasional cajoling to get things done. Great work on a job well done!

To Myles Morin, whose belief in the project from day one, and his corresponding support... it can only be described as phenomenal.

A big thank you to Ralph Duke in Amarillo Texas, for putting together a photo shoot on super short notice. Thanks for the pictures and the coffee!!

Todd Dean

To my Mom and Dad, who through phone calls and late night visits over coffee believed in this project more than anyone. (And I'm sure you weren't biased in any way!)

And to Ernest Barbaric, who has been a strong supporter, believer, and overall genius in helping me with all things electronic about the book, website, and everything else that requires a keyboard. Anyone who works with you should consider themselves lucky.

Foreword

It is not often that I get to read and introduce a book to the public that holds such powerful financial knowledge and advice. *More Money Than Month* is a handbook for all of those who have ever struggled financially. I've been there myself and in my early twenties struggled to find a way out of my financial circumstances. It was my own journey to financial freedom that lead me to help people all over the world uncover their potential.

I've known Todd Dean for some time and am impressed with his desire to really help people get on sound financial footing and find a way to make their dreams a reality.

I've found, and Todd Dean writes about the fact, that for most people it's not just about the money. It is about what money means to us and the assumptions and beliefs about money we have accumulated over time. Most of these beliefs aren't even ours and were absorbed from our parents and early experiences with money. It is these beliefs that convince us what we can or can't accomplish financially and most of the time they are not reality. No matter if you are a spender or a saver, this book will help you gain an understanding of the basics of sound finances and help you grow beyond what you currently know.

For more than forty years, I've helped people understand the principles of increasing their personal wealth and that begins by taking a realistic look at where you are and what you really want to accomplish. *More Money Than Month* is a great starting place to make some real decisions that will help you accomplish your financial goals. No fortune is made overnight, but it can happen much sooner than you ever imagine once you put these techniques to work. The real change starts within you, once you understand what your life can be like when you no longer worry about money. Make that decision right now and step into a life of financial freedom.

—**Bob Proctor**

Dedication

To Renia, Matt, and Alex. Even when times get challenging,
I know I can always count on you to be there for me.
I cherish that more than anything.

Contents

1. The Trouble with Money
—13—

2. Who Decided That?
—29—

3. You Are Here
—45—

4. Connect the Dots
—65—

5. Digging Out of the Pit
—77—

6. Credit and Interest
—93—

7. There's Advice, and Then There's Advice
—105—

8. I Am Investor—Hear Me Roar!
—119—

9. Two Steps Forward ...
—135—

10. It's Your Money!
—145—

Chapter 1

The Trouble with Money

We normally think of numbers as precise and accurate. Computers use numbers—binary code made up of zeroes and ones—to perform near miraculous mathematical calculations that can send astronauts into space, reproduce photographs, and let us share news with friends around the world via email. Machines that use numbers to make our lives easier and more orderly are everywhere, everything from microwave ovens to toasters to televisions with multiple screens.

So why, when it comes to money, are so many people's lives in total chaos? Money is nothing but the representation of value expressed in numbers. With computers, calculators, financial software, and ATMs at our disposal, money should be one of the things in life that we don't have to worry about.

Many experts cite money problems as the number one cause of divorce in America. The U.S. Commerce Department reported that Americans had a negative savings rate in 2005 and 2006. (This means that people spent everything they earned and then dipped into savings to spend more.) The Pew Research Center reports that 51 percent of people say they don't use a formal budget to organize their finances.

Clearly something about money confuses, bothers, or frustrates people. Financial chaos permeates people's lives, causing innumerable problems. Ask the average person about his net worth, and very few can tell you what "net worth" *means*, much less what his is.

With "hope for the best" a major part of their financial plan, most people live in an ongoing state of economic disorganization. They know few real facts about their income, debts, monthly expenses, or assets, and go with their assumptions or emotions. They live paycheck to paycheck and complain when there's "more month than money" as though it were a surprise.

Families often have multiple debit cards and checkbooks on the same bank account, and they don't discuss or keep track of spending. Then they become irate when the bank charges an overdraft fee. Their disorganization costs them overdraft fees, late fees, reconnection fees—fees the world charges those who don't have their financial house in order.

More Money Than Month

A tragic cost of the disorganization is the bills that don't get paid on time when the customer has the money in the bank. Through neglect or ignorance on the consumer's part, utility bills, credit card bills, mortgage payments, and various other debts multiply exponentially when payments are not made on time. Not only does this affect your current state of financial affairs, it also impacts your future finances in the form of a lower credit score, higher interest rates, and having to rent instead of buy your home because you can't qualify for a mortgage.

Most of us have heard stories of families who have unopened mail (most with cellophane windows) stacked on a table or stuffed out of sight in a drawer. What started as disorganization for these individuals has now escalated into a state of denial about their bills. Rather than simply open the envelope and pay the bill, they put it aside and out of mind.

Fair Isaac Corporation introduced the first broad-based credit scoring system in 1989. Since then, the FICO score has become a major part of our lives. Approval for loans, interest rates on credit cards, and even insurance rates can be based on the FICO score. One of the major effects of the chaos most people suffer in their finances is a drop in their credit score.

One of the components of the FICO score is payment history, which should set off an alarm in the minds of those people who continually pay their bills late. It is easy to think that getting "close" to the due date is okay and not that big of a deal. But your score will show late as late, no matter if it is one day late or twenty-nine days late. A series of late payments can send the credit score plummeting. When that happens, life becomes much more expensive for those who are already feeling the pinch. The good news is that if late payments affect you so negatively, then on-time payments can do just the opposite and help you start to turn things around financially.

One definition of the word *economics* is "unlimited wants in conflict with limited resources." Nowhere is this battle more evident than in the household where financial chaos reigns. Without knowing whether something is affordable or not (under their nonexistent budget), many families simply keep spending until they are out of money. Afterward, they find that they have bought something they *want* with money that could have been used to pay for something they *need*.

When chaos controls the checkbook, the family faces constant financial pressure. The adults worry about being behind on bills and not being able to afford the necessities of life, and the children worry because the adults are worried. The future is ignored completely while the family tries to get through today.

The permeation of financial chaos throughout the household affects everyone's emotional outlook. Pessimism about money dominates their thoughts, so they take little or no action to provide for the future. "What's the use?" becomes the financial slogan. Instead of optimism and looking forward to a bright future, the family sees nothing but bleakness and despair whenever they try to look ahead.

The financial pressure can eventually cause great stress on relationships, sometimes fracturing them beyond repair. Even when a couple manages to stay together and survive the worst, the strain from money problems can reduce the quality of that relationship. Disagreements and silent suffering over money mar what should be a happy partnership.

Friendships can be torn apart over problems that one or the other of the friends is having with money. One may feel free to keep borrowing from friends, creating an imbalance in the relationship. A person may feel obligated to spend money unwisely to fit in with the rest of the group.

It's apparent that something is going wrong when it comes to how most people handle their money. What's the problem? How have so many people gotten themselves into a financial straitjacket?

A major cause of financial chaos is the lack of understanding and education people have about money and how it works. Textbook definitions of money give a flat and common sense definition of what money is. Money is a resource, something that has to be allocated wisely and properly if we are to live our lives in financial security. Like any resource, money can't be wasted simply on what's in front of us at a given time. Only planning can ensure that money is put to maximum use. Hmmm. That sounds really good, but if it's so simple, then why don't we do it? The real reason is that money, to most people, isn't just a commodity to be traded or a resource to be used wisely. It's their security. And the lack of money undermines that security. It is not so much the fact that money is a resource that causes the issues—it's how it makes us feel about ourselves, our past, and our future.

This is why you see lottery winners who end up broke and destitute, and star athletes and celebrities who spend tens of millions of dollars with nothing to show for it. No one ever taught them how to handle money effectively, so they brought their financial chaos with them into millions, and those millions slipped away.

I have also seen clients with similar issues as far as what money means, but they have the opposite problem. They have been in save mode their entire lives and now have millions, but they refuse to spend a dime to enjoy life. One such client is a woman—I'll call her Margaret—who is seventy years old and has more than a million dollars in cash and securities. She phoned me recently to ask if she could afford to spend $1,800 to repair her bathroom! Unfortunately this woman will never enjoy all of that money that she and her husband worked for all of those years because her fear of "what if" keeps her from living the great life that she has earned. It is clear that how you think about money is the key to your ability to manage it effectively.

Not only is it important to understand what money represents for us, it is also important to understand how money works, and that takes a special kind of math. One of the greatest financial ideas ever created was *compound interest* (interest earned or paid on previous interest), which has a seemingly magical power to grow a sum of money in an exponential fashion. Unfortunately too many people don't even take the time to calculate their income and debts each month, let alone delve into the concepts that can literally make them wealthy—like compound interest.

Another part of the denial game for many people is the reluctance to create a budget and stick to it. So many people do not want to create a budget because of their insecurities and fears. They carry a load of guilt because they are not doing what they know they should be doing financially. Creating a budget would reveal the ugly truth, so they avoid the concept completely, hoping that they will get by.

The inability to construct a simple, accurate picture of their finances is a sign that a person has a psychological block about their finances. Money carries a lot of emotional weight, and it is difficult for some to confront the truth about their financial behavior. It is only when people shake off the baggage of financial misinformation that they have acquired from parents, teachers, friends, and past financial disasters that they are able to advance themselves financially.

Much of this financial information is conveyed with the best of intentions. Many baby boomers have sought to give their children what they had to work so hard for. While this may feel good in the short term, it tends to produce a sense of entitlement and lack of true knowledge of how money works. The children want the lifestyle and affluent perks their parents have—and they want them instantly. After these children are on their own, they experience tremendous chaos having to depend on Mom and Dad to bail them out time and again.

Baby boomer investors also have made the market a volatile and interesting animal. Previous generations invested for the long haul, but recent decades have produced a swarm of investors who want instant results and bail immediately on any stock that declines a small amount. In their quest to produce quick returns, they allow their frustration to produce emotional reactions to the market's movements instead of sticking with a long-term plan.

The psychological aspect of dealing with money dominates the waking hours for many. Money may mean security, it may mean status, it may mean accomplishment—it means different things to different people. There are even those who shop compulsively and impulsively, spending every dollar they have on whatever is in front of them. They show little discipline when it comes to money because the feeling that comes from spending comforts them in some way.

More Money Than Month

Even individuals who have demonstrated discipline in other areas of their lives don't necessarily have a strong grip on their finances. They may be in great physical condition, possible only after spending considerable time and effort exercising and eating right. They may have an immaculately clean home. However, when it comes to money, they experience the uncontrollable urge to do something that goes against their nature.

Certain lifestyles require a lot of financial maintenance, and this can produce peer pressure to appear wealthier than you are. Some people feel they have to wear the very best, most expensive clothing or jewelry. Others may feel they have to drive the nicest, newest car. They are unable to resist the pressure that their friends or family put on them to consume.

Others uncontrollably spend money on their hobbies because of peer pressure. If you belong to a cycling club, you don't want to have the shabbiest bike. Even if it is unspoken, there is still pressure on members of a particular group to measure up. Few people can resist that pressure.

Having spent many years in the investment world, I know that most people don't have financial problems because they are grappling with high-level financial decisions, such as whether to add to their long position on grain in the commodities market or buy more options of a particular stock. Most people have financial problems because of the small, seemingly insignificant decisions they make about money day in and day out. They habitually overextend themselves, forget to pay their bills on time, rack up fees galore, and don't save a penny for the future.

Reckless behavior is the main ingredient in the problems people have handling their money. They don't practice discipline or restraint in their spending, don't live within—or below—their means, or unrealistically aspire to an affluent lifestyle that may be unrealistic for them. Modern society seems to have forgotten the principles that our grandparents practiced: work hard, save, and plan ahead. Everyone wants everything right now, but all they are getting is a life full of stress and turmoil—and it doesn't have to be this way.

Almost every facet of society suffers the effects of financial chaos, and we hear about it every time we read a headline or listen to the news. If the economic outlook turns bleak, it can have a devastating effect on everyone, but especially on those who are just getting by and living on exactly what they earn. You may think that this is just one lower-paid strata of society, but large numbers of professional people, executives, and those who earn large salaries are as wrapped up in financial chaos as someone earning entry-level wages. Just because you make a great deal of money doesn't make you smart—it just allows you to make bigger mistakes.

However, if you make an average income and have a family, the financial pressure can compound when fixed expenses skyrocket. Higher costs for fuel, housing, and food add more pressure to an already strained financial situation, and these families don't have as many options for cutting back.

The family that has gotten into revolving debt—credit cards, signature loans, and other debt—find themselves stuck having to pay for items that they bought and consumed months, or even years, earlier. This happens frequently to individuals who buy something like a boat or recreational vehicle and then tire of it and sell it a few years later. Frequently they find that the item is now worth much less than what is left on the loan (often referred to as *upside down*), and they must still continue paying on something they no longer own or enjoy. This lack of financial discipline and understanding, combined with disorganization and almost no savings, creates a situation that could lead to disaster.

Those who suffer from financial chaos pay more for nearly everything they consume. Without spare cash, they're unable to take advantage of savings when unexpected bargains turn up, so they often put the purchase on a credit card, on which they may have an interest rate of 18 percent or more. This completely obliterates any bargain they feel that they made.

Add in fees, late charges, high interest rates, and other assorted costs associated with a low-cash, high-debt lifestyle, and suddenly they are paying more in finance charges than the cost of the purchased item. With a little organization and discipline, the same purchases could be made at a steep discount, instead of double or triple the original cost.

More Money Than Month

When consumers find themselves with less cash, they have fewer options when it comes to the products they can purchase. Because of the lower buying power they have, they tend to be more price conscious, considering items based entirely on price, rather than quality. In general (though not always), lower-priced items offer lower quality. The lower the quality, the more often items have to be replaced.

The continued choice of lesser-quality items because of lack of money leads to a downward spiral of buying power. Items must be replaced more often, and the consumer without enough cash winds up paying more for everything he owns because it is so frequently replaced. A good example of this is a couple who decide to purchase an inexpensive dining table and chairs for $1,200, rather than a better quality set for $4,000. What they don't realize is that the cheaper set will need to be replaced every five or six years, while the better quality set will last thirty years or more. And if you have to replace something in the future, you replace it at the inflated prices of tomorrow instead of the current prices of today.

This illustration was brought home to me a short time ago when some friends moved to a larger home and decided to donate their old dining table to charity because it was still in good shape but didn't fit the décor of the new home. The husband told me that the table and chairs had been purchased by his parents when he was six months old for $500—he had just turned forty-two. What a deal! Needless to say, my friend purchased a top-of-the-line dining set for the new house and is betting that it will still be around when he turns eighty.

The financial future is gloomy for those who are not organized and responsible with their finances. Unless they change their habits, they are confined to a lifetime of stress, anxiety, and living a lower quality of life than they should have to endure.

Additionally, the disorganized financial mess can make job prospects bleak for the person who is out of work. Employers frequently check credit histories of new applicants, and a low score can lead to either no job offers or lower-paying job offers. It is also much harder to acquire reliable transportation and keep the overall financial stress of life from interfering with your job.

For those who neglect their finances, the world is full of shortages. They dwell over the long list of items they want but can't afford. Food, clothing, furnishings for their home—there always seems to be something that is just beyond their financial reach. Thus they are never satisfied with what they can have.

This shortage—which is real—is paired with the never-ending desire for *more* that most modern consumers have. As the economy shrinks their buying power, the hunger grows, and the gap between what they want and what they can afford also grows. Their own financial weaknesses are magnified when the larger economy weakens.

Overall, a lagging economy lowers the standard of living for those who have lost control of their finances. They may cast blame at the various factors "out there," but the reality is that consumers must live on less if they have any hope to recover from the edge of financial ruin. They must accept responsibility, take control, and make a plan, which includes saving.

When a family is already in a white heat to spend everything they earn plus whatever else they can borrow, saving money is merely a concept, not a reality. What they find is that the future comes whether they save or not, and their financial situation gets worse. Like a series of dominoes falling, the wealth of the average family drops as one factor after another takes effect. From no control over spending to lack of financial knowledge to no savings, the situation starts to feed on itself, spiraling lower and lower until the family hits bottom financially.

The future is not something that most people contemplate on a daily basis. In fact, it's not even something they contemplate on a yearly basis. If the subject ever comes up, you'll hear them rationalize by saying that they are focused on the present, trying to get by from day to day. What they fail to realize is that tomorrow could be easier with prior planning, and it will inevitably be more difficult if no plan is put into action.

More Money Than Month

As baby boomers reach retirement age, a large wave of retirees who have not prepared for retirement are reaping the results of their lack of planning. At the time that they had hoped (note that I didn't say planned) to quit working and take it easy, they are forced to continue to work, and often the only jobs open to retired people are low-paying jobs. With just a little foresight, they could have invested in various retirement plans and arranged their finances so their later years would be easier. Instead of hoping to retire carefree, they could actually have done it.

Parents are also discovering that the college education they had planned for their children may now be out of their financial reach. Because they failed to allocate money for college when the children were younger, they are forced to admit that the children who want to enter college today are on their own as far as figuring out the financing. The fact that the parents are in such a chaotic financial state themselves precludes them from helping with college, and the odds are good that their children will embark on some of the same financial mishaps.

People grapple with day-to-day living, doing everything they can to get by. When they find themselves stuck financially, they blame the economy, the government, the tax system—they blame everyone but their own lack of organization. By failing to take care of their financial priorities, they let less important items take precedence. Their life is filled with less-than-best choices.

Housing itself becomes an issue. People often struggle with the rent or the mortgage payment. Sometimes they find themselves paying late, and charges and added interest eat into their payment. This adds to the number of payments or forces an additional amount to be paid the following month. The home, instead of being a refuge of comfort and warmth, becomes a dull ache—just another bill to be paid.

Then the unfortunate wage earner has to deal with the consequences of wages that seem to always be too little, combined with prices that never stop rising. The family sees their standard of living decline as they struggle to earn more money, not understanding that the amount of income is only one factor and that their financial habits are the real problem.

Everyone has a different attitude toward money. No socioeconomic class is without weakness in dealing with money. It is one of the unique problems of life that transcends every segment of society. People with high incomes are just as prone to overspend and undersave as people with low incomes.

Through advertising and other media, modern society has created an insatiable desire in the population to consume, creating a "need" even among those who are not the target market. The desire is so intense that people who see an item advertised don't consider the consequences of making the purchase, or they rationalize that they "need" it. This unquenchable desire spans all demographics, and it starts in childhood. How many times as a child did you see a commercial for the latest and greatest toy, a new Popsicle treat, or a box of Cap'n Crunch?

As mentioned earlier, the larger economy can play a big part in the downward spiral of a household's finances. Rising energy and food costs impact everyone, but those who are already struggling financially are hit harder. Without a budget, savings, or any coherent game plane, the disorganized household is at the mercy of the economic elements.

The impact of poor financial organization is felt by everyone in every category. Single, married, parents, childless, older people who are established, and younger adults who are still transitioning into adulthood—no one is immune from the effects.

Just as money can build on itself through compound interest, poor financial organization can compound a household's worries and concerns. It takes an ever-increasing toll on the mental state of everyone in the family. It can damage relationships, careers, and even lead to emotional or mental problems.

More Money Than Month

How do these issues compound? The situation is similar to an old nursery rhyme:

> **For want of a nail the shoe was lost.**
> **For want of a shoe the horse was lost.**
> **For want of a horse the rider was lost.**
> **For want of a rider the battle was lost.**
> **For want of a battle the kingdom was lost.**
> **And all for the want of a horseshoe nail.**

The moral of the nursery rhyme is that small details can escalate and become severe. The escalation is usually so gradual that by the time anyone knows something is wrong, it takes a monumental effort to recover, if you can recover at all.

For example, the lack of a working budget causes some people to be late paying their bills. They may have late payments or utilities shut off for nonpayment. Then they must pay extra to have them turned on again. The additional fees eat into the money for other bills, which in turn makes those late, thereby generating other charges. Eventually they miss a payment on something big—a vehicle or even the family home—and find themselves having to move or even declare bankruptcy.

All for want of a little financial organization.

Who is affected the most by this constant state of disorganization? First are those with little or no savings. They have no security because at any moment the washing machine can break down, or a child can get hurt and have to go to the emergency room, or one of a thousand different things that require money to fix can happen. People with no savings have to count on a perfect, problem-free life to get by.

Those who are in volatile careers also have to worry. If the job's pay varies quite a bit ("feast or famine")—sales jobs are notorious for this kind of lifestyle—then these people are affected more by disorganization. They have to put money back when times are good to cover for those times when things are not as good. That requires planning and foresight, both of which are learned skills and don't come naturally for most people.

Another group that is more likely to suffer when finances are disorganized are those who are at a transitional stage in their lives. Whether graduating from college, preparing to marry or divorce, moving to another part of the country, or changing jobs, unexpected expenses are always involved in the transition. Going through a transition is one of the key times when a person must be organized with his finances and plan carefully.

Essentially, anyone who expects to have a positive financial future needs to be aware of the exact state of his financial situation down to the penny—not sort of or kind of or close enough, but to the *penny*. Even those with high incomes must pay attention, or else they run the risk of spending the money just as fast as it comes in.

If a person lets financial issues affect him emotionally, it can cause problems in his relationships, both on the job and at home. If he is not careful, financial turmoil could affect his work performance, and thus his income.

The ability to save is jeopardized, as has been discussed earlier. The lack of savings increases the chance that a minor incident will blossom into a full-grown emergency because of the lack of money to resolve it quickly.

Investments may be part of a comprehensive financial plan for many people, but for the majority of consumers, putting any money away at all is a fantasy. Even for those who have investments, many times they could invest more if they had a better financial plan or would choose better investments that suited their particular needs instead of what someone else said they needed.

As we've seen, anything that relies on the FICO score or other credit score is affected by the financial chaos that people often find themselves in. It's the closest thing to the "permanent record" that so many of us were threatened with in grade school. This particular financial record, however, follows a person for years and reflects the results—the damage—that long-term disorganization can have on a person's credit report.

Along with the financial damage itself, disorganization and its effects wreak havoc on a person emotionally. His sense of security, self-esteem, and confidence are eroded by the sometimes humiliating situations that he may find himself in because of his money problems.

The stress of dealing with financial problems can even lead to physical ailments. In other words, you can literally be sick of worrying about money. The financial problems that most people suffer are not *money* problems—they are emotional problems. This is due to the fact that they have certain beliefs about how money works and what having it—or not having it—says about them as a person. It shows in our assumptions of our class status and socioeconomic background, all of which can be changed at any point, but most people don't even know to try.

The good news is that there are very few financial mistakes that you can't recover from, and after you learn how to fix the immediate problems, you also can learn the long-term solutions.

One person who I'd like to introduce you to throughout this text is a man named Charles. Charles is a client of mine from Toronto. Charles is a regular guy from a regular family. They were blue-collar, worked hard, and never had a great deal of money, but they managed. After high school, Charles started partying, drinking, and had occasional run-ins with the law. If anyone was in financial chaos, it was him, and things just got worse as his alcoholism escalated and was enhanced by substance abuse.

Even at the bottom of the pit, Charles knew he could get more from his life. He didn't want to be the black sheep whom everyone avoided and talked about at family gatherings. As his twenties slipped away, Charles could feel the clock ticking. He wanted to be the rock of his family—the one everyone could turn to when they needed help. So he decided to start digging his way out—and so can you.

Chapter 2
Who Decided That?

Every day we make thousands of decisions—what route to take to work, what to wear, what to say, paper or plastic, Coke or Pepsi—without consciously thinking about the decision-making process. If we had to go through a step-by-step process for each decision, two things would happen—we wouldn't get much done, and we would all be crazy from the stress. Our minds have developed shortcuts so we can make decisions instantly with no real input from the conscious part of our brains (and thus protecting our mental health).

What is the decision-making process? What steps is our mind actually going through when we decide to watch one movie instead of another?

In a logical decision-making process, we first establish a goal. The goal is the result we want after the decision is made. The goal might be "to get to work" or "to eat lunch." When the goal is as clear-cut as those two options, the first step is pretty simple. Sometimes our mind will wander, and our goal will become vague. If you've ever said, "I'm hungry, but I'm not sure what I'm hungry for," then you've experienced the slight confusion that surrounds having a vague goal.

After we have established our goal, we consider our options. We may have two options that we have to decide between, or we may have multiple options. This step alone can be difficult in modern society because we are faced with so many choices in so many areas of our lives. Supermarket aisles bulge with a wide variety of products. Cable and satellite television provides us with hundreds of channels, and the Internet offers unlimited access to anywhere in the world at a moment's notice.

When we go through the logical decision-making process, we can choose among options based upon what we think or feel might meet our goal. At this point we decide to gather data. Sometimes we base our decision on previously selected data—we've traveled to work before, so we know which routes are available. At other times we have to do research of some kind to get information. We may read reviews to decide which movie to watch. We look at the sky before going for a walk to see if we might need an umbrella.

We then take the data we've collected and compare it against the available options to see which option matches the information. Based upon that comparison, we make our decision and proceed with our choice.

All of this, of course, is based on *rational* decision making. Rational means that we use pure reason to weigh our options and choose the right path. Unfortunately, most of us don't make rational decisions most of the time. Sure, sometimes we follow Ben Franklin's advice and make a list comparing the benefits and drawbacks of the different options. Usually, however, we go with our gut feeling. We may flip a coin or cut a deck of cards or use some other random or coincidental occurrence. Or we may simply choose the first option that comes along that seems like it might accomplish the desired result.

Some people consult their horoscope (or private astrologer), tarot cards, the almanac, tea leaves, or some other esoteric resource. They may consult an expert and follow the expert's advice—sometimes even if the expert's expertise is in another realm entirely. (Expertise in one field often carries over, at least reputation-wise, to other fields.) How many times has a cardiologist been asked about a skin condition? We make a connection mentally, even though it really doesn't make much sense.

Making a rational decision implies some attempt at impartiality, to stand back and weigh the options objectively. Most people find that even if they try to be objective, especially about their finances, they just can't make objective decisions. This is not to say that they make the wrong decision, but they may make an emotional decision. All irrational decisions are not incorrect, and all rational decisions are not correct. But we usually use shortcuts when making decisions, sometimes even if the decisions are important to us. However, I think most of us would agree that the more important the goal, the more important it is that we use a rational process to make the decision.

What constitutes a rational decision? First of all, we need to make sure of our accuracy. Is the goal, the final result, what we are really trying to achieve? Do we have conflicting goals that we are trying to resolve with this one decision? Are we aiming to achieve the result we really want or the one we think we "should" be aiming for?

Gauging the various options can sometimes be hazardous. We are not always good choosers because of a lack of information, emotional bias, or a limited outlook. A rational process would have us look at all options that are legally, morally, and ethically viable.

If selecting all possible options is difficult, then collecting data is another level of decision making entirely. In today's society we are awash in a sea of information, not all of it good. We consult the Internet, which is infamous for incorrect and inaccurate information. We ask for advice from people who are not qualified to provide it. We consider irrelevant information as well as relevant and often give them equal weight. In a rational process, we would be more discriminating in the sources we used and trusted.

Finally in a rational decision-making process, our analysis would be clear-cut, methodical, and based on the facts. We would compare and contrast data, perhaps debate the issues, and then make the rational decision—which might still be incorrect, but the odds are better because we have thought it out logically. But when we don't consider the options and just go with our gut, it doesn't bode well for our long-term financial security.

This is heightened by our tendency toward last-minute decisions. It is well-known that we all have a heavier aversion to loss than we do to gain. If you look at your finances, you will react more strongly to someone stealing $20 than you will to someone giving you $100. The same is true in the investment world, no matter if that investment is your home or a particular stock. When you see the value of that investment on Monday, and it goes up by 5 percent on Wednesday, you will probably have a smile on your face for a short while and then put it in the back of your mind. But if that same investment loses 5 percent in those same two days, you're on the phone calling people in a panic! No one wants to lose what they have, but sometimes trying to hold on to every single dime by jumping out at the first sign of trouble actually costs you money in the long run.

Because there are no guarantees with investments, fear takes over. What most people don't realize is that there are no guarantees in anything; it is merely your perception that some things are safe and others are not. Fear can convince people to bury money in the backyard, refuse to use any type of credit, and never buy a home of their own. There is a happy medium, and it can be found through reasonable expectations and fear management. But this means we have to think about the problems, not just gloss over them.

Most of us are habitual when it comes to mental processes. Even so-called smart people make bad decisions out of habit. We may rationalize our lack of effort by downplaying the decision as unimportant. When it comes to decision making, many of us are like a child being forced to do his homework. Do we really want to do all of that research and comparison, or is it just easier to make the decision quickly and go with it?

Other times we are simply apathetic. Too many decisions between people involve one of the parties saying, "I don't care." This stance doesn't help the process; it simply puts the burden of the decision (and the consequences) on the other people involved. We simply don't want the burden of making a decision.

Sometimes a decision is made hastily because it was not approached with the appropriate sense of urgency or importance. Many important decisions are made on the fly because they were put off until the last minute. Most of us are guilty of procrastination at various times. Decisions made in haste are often regretted later.

Procrastination in decision making is most often the result of fear. One of the most common fears—and least discussed—is the fear of making a wrong decision. We may fear the consequences or the responsibility of a decision we have to make, so we put it off. More often than not, the fear we have is misguided, and a second-best solution is better than no solution. If the question to be decided is very important, though, we will often delay until outside forces compel us to make the decision.

If we acknowledge that our decision-making process is faulty, then how did we come to make decisions this way? What influences created this situation?

The most significant influence, of course, was our parents. Especially when we were younger, our parents naturally exerted a tremendous amount of influence over every aspect of our lives. It went beyond verbal advice, though. As children we picked up on every nuance and hint that our parents indicated. If they spoke admirably of a financial decision that an uncle or grandfather had made years before, that tone seeped into our subconscious to be used later when making a similar decision.

Our siblings also had a great effect on our decision making. An older brother or sister may have been the first one to show us how to draw straws to make a decision. If we were ever bullied or hurried by an impatient sibling, it may lead us to hurry decisions now for fear of the repercussions of taking too long.

Friends and playmates showed us how to make decisions. If we ever catch ourselves as adults saying, "Eenie, meenie, minie, moe …" when making a decision, then we acknowledge that the influence of our childhood friends still carries weight with us.

To children *everyone* is an authority figure. Teachers, principals, policemen—all adults are assumed to have authority of some kind. When we watched an adult make a decision, maybe even articulating the reasoning, we internalized the idea that *that* was how decisions were made.

As adults we still labor under the influences of our childhood, but now we have added influences. Our family still directs us in many ways, even if we don't interact with them as much as we did when we were younger. Siblings may have gained expertise or success in some area that adds weight to their advice.

A major influence on the decisions we make is our spouse or significant other. It's appropriate and proper for two people to consult with one another to reach a decision that affects both of them. Many times, however, one personality will be stronger than the other and dominate the process. The more passive partner may completely abandon the process for the decision, fearing conflict or confrontation.

More Money Than Month

As working adults, our co-workers have a tremendous influence on us. We often spend more waking hours with fellow employees than with our families. That amount of time has a decided effect on us. Just as when we were younger, we may face peer pressure about certain decisions that we make.

Often we add weight to advice given to us by a minister, pastor, or other spiritual adviser. We may believe that they have a connection to a higher power, giving them insight to decisions that the rest of us lack. They may advise that we pray or meditate about a decision before making it.

Finally, of course, we have the option of consulting professionals in the field. We consult lawyers, bankers, stockbrokers—we may even ask the grocer about what fruit to buy. Asking professionals for advice is a good idea if they are competent and if they have *our* best interest, rather than their own, in mind.

If we go into a furniture store and ask questions about quality or value, then of course *their* furniture will offer the best quality and value. Why else would they be in business? (The answer: They may be, *ought* to be, in business to make money.) The furniture salesman's goal is to make money by selling you furniture. If this coincides with your desire to get the best quality and value, then fine. But even if his interests and yours don't coincide, he will recommend his store's furniture because *he looks out for his own interests first.*

When it comes to investing, it becomes hard to accept advice even from qualified professionals because we are so emotional about money. We hear on the news that we're supposed to average a 10 percent return. If we only get 8 percent, we immediately think that we should fire our investment adviser and that they aren't looking out for us. They may actually be doing an excellent job if that year the broader market only made 7 percent. It is important to compare apples to apples and to apply your logical reasoning so you don't make a mistake that could cost you a tremendous amount of money in exit fees to move to a different adviser.

When it comes to money and investing, we possess certain ideas that affect our behavior as investors. We have the ideas, concepts, and beliefs that we were raised with, of course. If you were fortunate enough to have a parent who was a stockbroker or financial analyst, then you may have learned how to evaluate investments properly and objectively, using professional-level tools. More than likely though, even if you had a financial professional for a parent, he instilled his own investment biases in you, so you still have a difficult time being objective.

Most of us grew up in households that did not include an expert in finance. Regular people make decisions about investing in the same way that their parents did. What we learn early in life stays with us a long time. We may consider investing as putting money into a piggy bank. Some people may think of buying things as an investment. Some households value cash; others value items such as collectibles or other tangible items as investments.

Some households may determine that all the investing they can do is to put food on the table. When we have been raised a certain way, sometimes the information we retain is useful, but many times it's not.

The ideas about money that we were raised with affect—and cloud—our ability to make rational decisions when it comes to investing. Regardless of how our family thought of money when we were growing up, it's important that we try to have a healthy attitude about it as adults. If we discount the importance of money entirely or place more importance on it than it deserves, that is not a healthy attitude.

Some people regard money as a necessary and useful commodity, while others regard money simply as evil. Many families have developed ideas of morality around money. Some people live by the often misquoted saying, "Money is the root of all evil." (The actual quote is a verse from the Bible: "For the love of money is the root of all evil.") If a household considers money evil, it will be hard to develop much enthusiasm for earning, spending, and investing it.

Other families develop the opposite attitude, that money is the best way to judge people. They believe that only people with money—and who show it off—are worth knowing or being around. It is important to understand that money is simply a commodity of exchange—it does not necessarily mirror a person's value. Relationships based solely on money tend to be shallow.

Other influences that may affect us today are when families make decisions based on their finances. For example, a parent may teach her children never to lie, yet keep the money if a cashier makes a mistake and gives her extra change. A white lie may be okay if she can get a better price when she sells something. Such an inconsistent philosophy only confuses decision making when it comes to investing and finance.

Often our parents simply give us wrong economic information. They may honestly believe that "bonds are the only good investment," or "Japanese cars are always better." If we grow up believing such opinions—why wouldn't we, they came from our parents—then we base many of our decisions on inaccurate and misleading information.

Even if our parents gave us good information when we were children, it may not apply today. Economic conditions change along with everything else in the world. At one time it might have been a good idea to invest in a particular company, only to find that today new technology has rendered the company obsolete.

Our spouse's impact cannot be underestimated either. It is very common for your spouse to have not only different ideas about money, but completely opposite ideas, which can be a source of friction. I have a couple of clients named Jeff and Amy. Amy comes from an affluent family, and Jeff has done well, but it has all been on his own because his family was quite poor. The couple drives matching Mercedes sedans. One source of contention is the fact that Jeff keeps his car meticulously clean and is constantly irritated that Amy's is always trashed. He frequently finds French fries, paper cups, toys, and half empty bottles of water strewn about the floorboards.

Although I could see the problem immediately, Jeff was dumbfounded about why his wife cared nothing for the upkeep of her car. To me, this illustrated the vast difference in their mind-sets about money. Amy was raised with money, so she sees it as a commodity, and her car is an extension of that—it merely gets her from one point to another. That's it. Jeff, on the other hand, sees his car as a symbol of his success and the status that he has gained by hard work, so he sees it as an extension of himself—not just a ride to work.

Though the example of Jeff and Amy is unique, this same issue is played out in homes across the country as couples have to decide: Which purchases are priorities and necessities? Who drives which car and for what reasons? Do you set the thermostat on 75 or 65? And odds are you merely follow what you saw as a child instead of consciously choosing the right answer for your own family.

In today's world, the media also carry a great deal of weight when it comes to our attitude about money and investing. Commercials are designed to create a hunger in us for the products that they advertise. Extensive research is conducted to find out how to make consumers want the latest car, the tastiest potato chip, or a particular investment class.

Television and movies become the standards by which we judge our lifestyle. The lone hero takes on the villain and his army of henchmen, and only through a foolhardy but courageous gamble is he successful in winning. We internalize the message "gambling = winning." That type of philosophy is best left to Hollywood, but unfortunately the message is communicated, and we use it as a reference. The real message should be "educated risk = educated reward."

We also begin to believe that the lifestyles we see on television shows are what "everyone else" does. In other words, we assume that the fictionalized world we see is the reality for other people, even though it bears little or no resemblance to our own life (or anyone else we know). When we see characters drink a particular drink or wear a particular item of clothing, we feel pressure to emulate them. We try to live our lives as though we were on television.

We may also perceive the message in the news that "everyone" is going after a particular toy at Christmastime, or selling or buying a particular stock because it's popular or hot. We tend to want to be part of the latest trend or fad, even when it comes to financial matters. Infomercials blur the line between hucksterism and documentary. Supposed "experts" tout the benefits of whatever product they are pitching but rarely disclose their own financial interest in doing so.

So what is the message that we receive through the media? The number one message is *consume*. We are confronted with commercials between television programs and product placements during shows. Loud music, flashing lights, and pretty models communicate to us that we will be prettier, healthier, thinner, and better smelling if only we will use their product.

On the news we may hear how well or poorly the economy is doing. Polls tell us how difficult it is for the average person to make ends meet. We form our judgment based on what we see on the news, regardless of how we are doing personally. Increasingly the media use polls as news, and we form an opinion from that information, though polling is really only a very small and very inaccurate means of measuring opinions.

We may try to watch news programming to get a better idea of what is going on. Experts on a panel argue back and forth about what is happening and why. Keeping in mind that so-called experts usually have their own agendas, we are forced to try to decide on a matter when even the experts disagree.

When it comes time to invest our money, we are battling many influences that can steer us wrong. We may have developed habits that conflict with our goals as investors. Those habits can hinder our progress or even derail it completely. Most of those habits are some form of pain aversion. We'll do nearly anything to avoid pain, and saying no or cutting back hurts. It doesn't really hurt, but it forces us to make a conscious decision when it's much easier to make those decisions on autopilot. However, if autopilot isn't getting you where you want to be, then it's time to take back control.

This autopilot may be in the form of investing in only one thing, like CDs. While CDs have their place in the investment world, if you start when you are young and only invest in CDs, earning an average of, say, 3 percent over the long term, then you have missed out on a tremendous amount of return.

This doesn't mean you should go all in. Some investors are willing to trust chance when it comes to making investment decisions. They shoulder extreme risk while hoping for the big score. They trust their gut instincts about a company, a stock, or an industry and base their judgment on random occurrences that do not necessarily reflect reality over the long term.

Other investors have developed the habit of throwing money into a bad situation, refusing to stay informed about their investments. They make a decision and stick with it, regardless of the evidence that may accumulate showing the error of the decision.

Many people, wanting to play with the big boys, invest at a level that is way above their personal risk tolerance. For some, their personal finances may be so shaky that they should not be investing in anything bigger than a book on household budgeting. The question they need to ask themselves is, "Should I be rolling the dice in investments when I'm up to my neck in debt?"

When it comes to finances, the bad ideas outnumber the good ones.

Other investors have the idea of getting rich quick. Even those who make an occasional "quick kill" in a particular investment usually don't make money in the long run. There's an old saying, "There's no such thing as a free lunch." The truth is that most fortunes are earned through hard work, application of accurate knowledge, and patience. If you wonder how your own behavior stacks up, ask yourself, "If I continue this behavior, how will I feel and look in ten years?"

Some investors personalize the economy, as though fate only looks at one person. They may believe that if they buy a particular stock, it will go down for sure. Without going into advanced investment strategy, I'll offer this one useful piece of information: *The stock doesn't know you own it.* Making decisions based on the fear that some supernatural force will be influenced by your investments is not rational. But many use it as it an excuse to never save and then never risk—and as a result, they never get ahead.

What are some *bad* investment ideas? One is basing your investments on emotion and expecting a consistent return. Often the emotion in question is *desperation*, which is never a good state of mind to be in when making investment decisions. The decision is made based on hope rather than good knowledge.

Another bad idea is to make investments that are incompatible with your goals. For example, it would be unwise to invest money for your child's education in a high-risk venture. If you have properly analyzed your goals, then there is an appropriate investment among the hundreds or thousands of possibilities.

An investor has to consider his temperament when considering investments. Some people have very little tolerance for risk, so it would make little sense for them to invest in something that carries high risk. They worry that what they would have to endure would be worse than what they might gain financially. Again, there is a broad spectrum of possibilities to fit nearly any temperament.

Although advisers make the argument that rational investment decisions are the best way to go, many investors continue to make their decisions irrationally. They believe they are one type of investor when their behavior shows them to be something completely different.

I know an investment adviser, let's call him Dustin, who will tell you that he is a calm, rational investor—and he is until the market goes down. Then he panics and sells his positions. I've seen it time and again, but he will still tell you he is unemotional in his decision making. Even financial advisers have issues with regard to money. They can tell you how to do it, but that doesn't mean they can do it. That's how strong our programming about money is—it can override all you know to be true. It's also a warning to be very wary of appearances because the guy giving the advice may not be taking it.

Some people conduct themselves based on their fear of regret. They become so attached to the price of a stock, for example, that even when it goes down drastically, they hesitate to close the position because they are afraid that the price will go back up and they will miss out on the profit. Or a stock may even go *up* dramatically, and they will refuse to sell because it might go up even further and they will not earn the extra profit.

An investor may also base his decisions on previous results. A stock may have earned a lot of money in the past, and the investor sticks with it even if a smaller profit is logical under current economic conditions. Instead of taking a small profit, which would be the best decision given the market, he longs for the higher profit of yesterday.

No one wants to lose money on an investment, but some investors cling to a loser because they have an *excessive* aversion to losing. To avoid a loss, they put off making a decision until the bottom has dropped out completely.

Other times investors are influenced too heavily by recent news and trends. A stock may traditionally be a good performer but—as with any investment—a cycle may occur when the stock performs more moderately or falls some. Those who depend on current news may overreact and get rid of what is basically a healthy investment because they are scared of a temporary downturn.

One of the most common irrational behaviors is the practice of following the crowd, often against common sense. The headlines may scream that a particular investment is great and that "everyone" is putting their money into a particular business, stock, or industry. In the rush to follow the crowd, a type of lunacy takes over. Rational thought is cast aside.

More Money Than Month

Scottish journalist Charles Mackay wrote about the phenomenon in 1841 in his book *Extraordinary Popular Delusions and the Madness of Crowds*: "Men, it has been well said, think in herds; it will be seen that they go mad in herds, while they only recover their senses slowly, and one by one!"

Chapter 3

You Are Here

Todd Dean

The journey of a thousand miles begins with a single step.

Most of us have heard the saying written above whenever we have started a big project. When it comes to our personal finances, however, the average reaction is, "I have to *walk* a thousand miles? All by myself?" Luckily, the road to organizing your finances is considerably less than a thousand miles long. However, the point of the saying is correct—you have to start somewhere. You have to have a plan.

Why is having a plan so important? First of all, most of us intuitively understand that having a plan—even a plan that is second best—is better than having no plan at all. A plan provides a sense of direction to our actions. Fewer resources such as time and energy are wasted.

Planning also gives us a sense of control over our world. If you are satisfied with your financial situation after looking at it systematically, then you have confirmed your plan. On the other hand, if you realize that your finances are out of control, then creating and executing a plan can create order out of chaos. Most of the factors of our financial lives are within our control, if only we exert the control that we already have.

Having a plan also helps alleviate any fears we have about tackling something as full of emotion as our finances. A plan is simply a series of steps. When we start out thinking about our entire financial picture—especially if we already know we're in trouble—the problems can loom as large as a mountain. Reducing the issue down to manageable steps makes the entire process easier to accept and implement.

Let's go back to Charles's story. Charles started at the bottom with just a decision to change his life. That doesn't mean he woke up the next day and things were great. They weren't. He started by joining Alcoholics Anonymous. It was hard. He had debts, no assets at all, and very little education or job skills. The one thing he did have was determination. He worked hard and started saving small amounts. He made the commitment that he wouldn't touch that savings—no matter what—and he didn't. He started working in a multilevel marketing company and slowly made gains.

More Money Than Month

He said there was a time when he had to choose—$100 for groceries or $100 for a room to hold a seminar—and he chose the seminar. He invested in his future and endured the pain of the present knowing it would pay off. This is one point that many people overlook. He endured the short-term pain for long-term gain—and very few people want to do this.

For some people, getting organized is difficult because of the fear they always experience when they think seriously about money. As a society, we are poorly trained when it comes to money, and the unfamiliar always provokes fear. The only thing we usually know about our finances is that they're a mess. It's not uncommon for a person to simply shake his head and say, "I don't want to think about it."

If you've decided to overcome that fear and get serious about your finances, then it will help to think of the process as a series of steps—very *small* steps. Ease into the process, and your comfort level will tell you when you're getting close to something important. What you will usually find is that even if your situation is bad, getting a clear picture of it will lessen your fear.

When trying to assess your financial picture, you need to understand some financial terms. Your financial picture has two components—*cash flow*, which is how much money you have available for various purposes, and *net worth*, which is how much cash you would have if you liquidated all of your assets and paid off all of your debts.

The first step to organizing your finances is to figure out your monthly cash flow. Cash flow is an important factor because it is the basis for all of your investment goals. Only by having a positive cash flow—money left over after paying your monthly bills—can you hope to begin investing and become wealthier.

To figure out where you are financially, you have to gather some materials. You'll need something to write on, of course, and something to write with. You'll also need a calculator. All of this can be done using computer software, but family discussions are often more productive around a dinner table, and the pen and paper are much more portable. However, use what works best for you.

The next step is to gather your financial records. Your tax return from the previous year will be useful, as well as any recent paycheck stubs. Collect bank statements and any monthly bills you have. Print out the latest information online for your accounts so you have up-to-the-minute information on what is being spent. Organization is also very important for this process, so having some sort of folder, large envelope, or expandable file where you can store these records while you work on your cash flow analysis and financial plan is helpful. Until you are confident that you have your monthly cash flow under control, keep your records in the file when you're not working on them. You're practicing "fuzzy finance."

After you've gathered your records, you need to assign a time to work on your finances. Make an appointment with yourself and your family to discuss finances. It's important that you choose a time when you will not be interrupted or distracted. Even if money is not the most important thing in your life—and it shouldn't be—keeping your finances straight and feeling good about them is important to your and your family's well-being. Set aside the time for something this important.

Before you start your first session, take a deep breath. Don't let this first step intimidate you. Remember, *it doesn't have to be perfect*. Don't get so hung up on a small detail that you stop the whole plan. Take the process seriously and do the best you can, and you'll be all right. As you go along, you can make necessary adjustments to your figures and estimates.

Having said that, try to be as accurate as you can. You're creating a picture of your financial reality, and you want that picture to be as close as possible. Use your records as resources to ensure accuracy. For the numbers for which you don't have records, make your estimates as close to accurate as possible. For instance, if you are trying to figure out how much your electricity bill might be for an upcoming month, see if you have last year's bill for the same month. With rising energy costs, this year's bill will probably be higher than last year's, even if your usage is the same. So estimate an increase in the bill that sounds reasonable. Don't agonize that it's not exact; simply do the best you can in a case like this.

However, you should have some idea of a realistic figure. One of the mistakes many people make is to write down what they *think* they are spending. For example, if asked how much you spend on lattes every month, you may say about $50. They cost $5.50 each and you think you get one of these beverages about two or three time per week. But when you look at the actual expenses, you find you get one three to four times per week, and your actual coffee expense is about $75. It seems a small difference, but we tend to underestimate what we spend in almost every area. The correct amount can make a big difference on a monthly basis, so do your best to be accurate.

From this point on, keep detailed records of your money. Keep receipts, paycheck stubs and bank statements, bills, and anything else that might be helpful. Analyzing your cash flow is an ongoing process, and future sessions will be easier if you have proper records to work with.

Cash flow is made up of two ingredients—income and expenses. The first step—the *fun* step—is collecting your income information. You likely have one or more types of income—wages from your job (including bonuses), interest on a savings account, profits from selling items, maybe dividends or other income from investments you already own, or income from a partnership or business. Economists have various classifications for income, but for the purpose of establishing cash flow, *income* is defined as "money available to help pay your bills."

What you want to do is establish your monthly income. If you have an irregular income (you may be in sales, for example), use the average of your salary for the previous three months. If there is an anomaly during that period—an extremely high or low amount—use your tax return and figure out your average per month. Don't agonize over being exact—this is one of the instances where you can get as close as possible. It may help to look at your bank statements and analyze the deposits to get an accurate picture.

Remember to use only take-home pay for your numbers. Although you earn more, the money you pay in taxes is not available to pay your bills. Also, if you receive large annual bonuses, that money will not be available to use the whole year (unless you save it and portion it out monthly—a smart idea).

What we're trying to discover is the typical month's income. Also include any maintenance payments you receive—child support, spousal support, alimony, government checks, etc. You want to account for every penny that comes into the household.

At the top of your paper, write "Income." Underneath it list the different sources of income you receive and the amounts. When you have worked through all of your income to the best of your ability, add up the numbers to find the total. (Worksheets are provided at the end of this chapter to help with this accounting.)

When you see the total, does it look realistic? Does it seem to reflect how much money you have to work with each month? If the answer is no, go back and see if you have missed something. Make sure you didn't count something twice or use a quarterly or annual amount instead of a monthly average. Check to see if you have included every source of income you receive.

If the figure for your monthly income looks right, then it's time to move to monthly expenses. Trying to calculate your monthly expenses can make you crazy if you let it, so go easy on yourself and take it a step at a time. Although it may look like a mountain of bills to you, it's simply the total of various categories. Figuring one category at a time makes the stack much more manageable.

First, think about the money you spend on necessities—food, clothing, and shelter. The shelter category is usually the largest, so tackle it first, and everything else will seem much smaller. This, of course, is your mortgage or rent payment. If your insurance and property taxes are included in your payment, leave them in. If you pay those separately, add them to the category. Remember to calculate a monthly average.

Next are your utilities. Include everything that goes into the home. That may include any or all of the following: electricity, gas, water, garbage collection, telephone (both landline and cell phone), Internet, satellite or cable television, cleaning services, and landscaping. Also add any fees paid to condominium or homeowners associations.

After housing, total up your food expenses. I usually have people separate food expense into two categories: what you spend on groceries and what you spend at restaurants. This gives you a good idea of eating in versus eating out. Although we all must eat to live, you choose where you eat and how much you spend. The eating-in expense tends to be a regular expense, while eating out is a variable expense. When you have totaled both types of food expenditures, decide if you want to include toiletries and other personal items that you purchase at retail outlets other than the supermarket. With today's superstores, many people purchase all of their household items at the same store.

After you have entered your items in this category, look it over carefully to make sure you haven't forgotten anything. Again, be realistic—don't short your food budget just to make it look better. Most people don't keep receipts from restaurants or the supermarket, so use your bank records or any other records to come up with a somewhat accurate dollar amount.

Next list your clothing budget. Again, be realistic about what you spend on clothing; don't be judgmental or critical of your habits. This may be a category where you don't spend money every month, so calculate how much you spend over a year and divide by twelve.

After food, clothing, and shelter, the next major category is transportation. If you take public transportation, include bus, subway, or taxi fares and any other expenses you have. If you own a car, you have multiple items to list. You have the car payment if your car is not paid for. You also need to list your auto insurance, registration, licenses and taxes, parking fees, and other permits for your vehicle usage. Add fuel and maintenance (tires, oil changes, etc.), plus any other fees or charges you incur to use your vehicle.

Some of your auto expenses may have to be totaled for the year and then averaged. However you calculate them, try to include all of your expenses related to your auto ownership and usage. After the home, the vehicle is one of the largest expenses in the normal household. The Victoria Transport Policy Institute estimates that the average motorist devotes nearly 20 percent of the household budget to automobile costs.

After transportation, add your insurances (but not auto insurance, which was included above) and medical expenses. The insurance should be straightforward—life, dental, medical, and any other insurances that you carry. Enter doctor visits, prescriptions, and any medications that you buy regularly.

One note on insurance—this is not a place to save money by cutting it out. While you may reevaluate some of your coverage, being underinsured can be disastrous. One of my friends has a brother who is a surgical tech at a Texas hospital. He is one of those people who lives paycheck to paycheck, and he's never paid much attention to insurance. He has child support payments to his first wife and supports a second wife and little girl. During his first few weeks of work, it was raining lightly, and he left as usual on his Harley. The back tire slipped, flipping him over the handlebars and dislocating his shoulder. He was unable to work for three months, and because he had declined the short-term disability offered by the hospital, he was without pay for more than two months. His family went from living comfortably to filing for bankruptcy in less than three months. How much was the insurance? $5.43 every two weeks.

After you have your insurance and medical listed, next enter any payments you make on debts and loans, such as credit cards, department stores, furniture and appliance loans—anyplace that you are contractually bound to make payments. If you are behind on payments, put down the amount that you are *supposed* to pay each month. With credit products that don't have a fixed payment each month (such as credit cards), put down the minimum payment required. This doesn't mean you should make only the minimum payment, but we'll deal with that later. For now, just write in the minimum payment amount.

If you put a certain amount into savings each payday—and you should—add that to your list. Although you still have access to the money, it is better to treat it as an expense and budget around it. You should not be dipping into your savings regularly. Treat money that you put into investments the same way—as an expense. You pay yourself first, and this is a good habit, even if saving isn't something you have really done in the past. When we're adults, we can look back and evaluate how our parents handled money. Did they do well and have a tidy sum set aside, or do they still live right on the brink? For years my parents have lived on the brink, as do many people their age. That worked for them in their thirties and forties while they were raising children. But now they are in their sixties, and the idea of retirement is a frightening prospect. Don't let this be you.

Back to the cash flow. Now the categories get tougher because each individual has unique expenses. Be as detailed as you can now so you can better analyze the results later. Look for expenses such as haircuts, babysitters, lessons for the children (piano, singing, ballet), school expenses (tuition, supplies, books, fees), gifts (birthdays and Christmas), subscriptions, and organization dues.

Be sure to account for any allowances or pocket money—cash that is not designated for anything other than personal use. This is a difficult category for some people, because usually one or more members of the household have unfettered access to the cash and do not have to answer for how it was spent. If that's the case, then it's time they were held accountable. Whatever the amount is, it needs to be written on the list. Remember, *every dollar of income must be designated to some category.*

You should know your expenses better than anyone else, so categorize them as you need to in order to make it more organized for yourself. Beware the temptation not to count hidden expenses, such as daily stops at the coffee shop, trips to the snack bar or vending machine at work, treats, or regular shopping trips.

At the end of your cash flow analysis, every dollar of your take-home pay should be accounted for. If there is a gap (more income than expenses), yet you don't have extra money in your account, look at your spending again and see where the money goes. You may find that you've forgotten some expenses, or you may need to increase the amounts that you spend in the existing categories. Regardless, account for every dollar in every one of your categories.

On the other hand, the gap may be the opposite, meaning that your income is less than your expenses—you go into the red each month. Recheck your figures to make sure you haven't added something twice or exaggerated how much you spend in a category. If, after checking your numbers, you find that your expenses are more than your income, then you have a picture of your situation, and it reflects the need for some changes.

This is where the dreaded "B" word comes into play for many people—*budget*. But I don't like the word budget because most people just use it as an excuse for rearranging what they are already doing—which if that were the case, then they would be in total control of their finances. What you really need to do is prioritize—decide what is really important for you to spend money on given the goals you say you want and then cut the rest out. That's right—I said cut it out. Don't keep doing the same thing, or you will get the same results. Change your habits; don't just shuffle them around.

If you did your cash flow analysis and found that there is extra money at the end of the month, then this is the amount you have to invest. If you want to invest more, then you have to (1) increase your income, (2) decrease your expenses, or (3) both.

If you wound up with more expenses than take–home pay, the answer is the same, only more urgent. You must take the extra step of becoming solvent in your monthly cash flow, or you will never be able to invest anything. You must increase your income or decrease your expenses, and your best bet is to do both.

If you want to increase your income, look first at your present job. Can you get an increase in pay somehow, maybe by gaining a particular certification or getting a degree? Can you work longer hours to get a bigger paycheck or work harder to produce more (particularly if you work on commission)?

You may choose to take a second job to increase your income. Many successful people with good incomes also sell real estate, work part time in retail or restaurants, or moonlight using their job-related skills to earn extra money as a consultant. If you want to increase the amount you can invest, increasing your income is one way to do it and see immediate results.

If you also need to decrease your expenses, look first at the "phantom" expenses. Does a large share of your income go out through the pocket money or "unknown" category? If so, a lack of financial discipline may be crippling your ability to get ahead. Designate a certain dollar amount as allowance, and then stick to that amount. Put the cash in an envelope in your house, and when it's gone, have the discipline to say no more. The person who does the majority of the "unknown" spending must be held accountable for staying within that budgeted amount. It is impossible to make progress until you stop the bleeding. Do whatever you have to do. You know how you set your alarm clock twenty minutes ahead so you'll get up on time? If you need to remove $500 from your checkbook so you don't see it, but you still know it's there, then do it. Whatever mind games work for you, use them.

If you have a lot of revolving debt, such as credit cards, you must control their use until you can get them paid off, or at least paid down to a manageable amount. After you have revolving debt lowered or eliminated, *stop using it*. Too many people use their credit cards for eating at restaurants or for other consumable expenses, only to wind up financing their meals for months or even years. These types of financial habits are the root of the financial chaos in many people's lives. Addressing that root cause is essential for real change.

For those who have a negative cash flow, more extreme measures must be taken. A negative cash flow will eventually cause your entire financial house to come crashing down around your ears. You must take action! For example, how much are you spending on vehicles? Do you have more than one? Do you *need* more than one? If the answer is yes, as it is for many families these days, do you *need* the particular types of vehicles you now drive?

"Need" is the operative word here, because most of us confuse our *wants* with our *needs*. You may have been living a lifestyle beyond your means, and this may be reflected in your choice of ride. Big SUVs can be truly necessary for large families, but how many people fall into that category? It's time to take a look at your life priorities and see if you have been spending money simply to maintain a certain status. If you have, then get ready for a shock, because one way or another it will all end. It's far better to lower your lifestyle voluntarily than to have collection agencies, bank foreclosure, and bankruptcy do it for you.

I will explain the consequences of debt in a later chapter, but for now you must work diligently to get your cash flow under control. Look at ways you can make your income and your expenses balance.

There are often a couple of obstacles to making these changes. The first is being maxed out on virtually everything. This is where you have to make some tough choices. Do you move to a less expensive home? Do you get a second job? Do you say no to all of those activities that aren't really moving you toward your goal? Face the pain and make those tough choices sooner rather than later. Accumulating fees can also keep people feeling as if they are trapped. One of the few things that can help reduce these fees is more cash flow. You've got to get rid of some of the debt and fees, and the only way to do this is to get rid of the debt and late payments. You may feel like it's not possible to get a second job, but very few people couldn't work somewhere in the evenings or on weekends if they wanted. And that's the key phrase—if they wanted.

As mentioned earlier, *net worth* is how much you would have left if you sold everything you own at fair market value and paid off all of your debts. Most people are shocked at how small their net worth truly is. Depending on how you spend your money, you may be shocked at the answer too.

To discover your net worth, first list all of your assets—all bank accounts, investments, real estate, cash value of life insurance, household items such as electronics and appliances, jewelry, collections, vehicles (including boats, motorcycles, or any other recreational vehicles), and all other possessions. Again, it may be difficult to get exact numbers, but estimate the value of these items as closely as you can. You may need to make some calls to find out the value of jewelry or collectibles, for example, but this is a process that takes time. Use the time to refine your numbers so you have as accurate a picture as possible of your assets.

Remember that the cash you have in your bank accounts may be about to go out in the form of payments on bills. Don't fool yourself into thinking you have more assets than you do if you haven't paid your bills yet. Having your utilities on is not an asset.

After you've totaled the value of your assets, do the same thing with all of your debts and obligations. Use the payoff amounts on vehicles, real estate, and various loans. These figures may be easier to be accurate with because you can get the numbers from the companies and institutions that you owe the money to. Again, put the numbers on your list.

Many people are shocked at the fact that their vehicles are worth so little, especially when they owe more than the vehicles are worth. This is known as being *upside down* on a debt. Even new cars are notorious for depreciating quickly after they are driven off the dealer's lot.

Subtract the total of your debts and obligations from your total assets and you have your net worth. If this is a positive number, then congratulations—you can focus on investments that will build it faster. If the answer is a negative number, then you know where you stand and which obligations are the most cumbersome.

Many people confuse *income* with *wealth,* but that's a mistake. If you make $100,000 per year and spend all of it without saving any, then you are not wealthy. You're simply living a lifestyle that is not meeting your long-term goals. Wealth is measured in net worth. Being upside down in your net worth is not unusual for many people in today's spendthrift society, especially for young families.

In their book *The Millionaire Next Door,* Thomas Stanley and William Danko devised a formula to determine if a person was wealthy based on the person's net worth. To be considered wealthy, they said, "Multiply your age times your realized pretax annual household income from all sources except inheritances. Divide by ten. This, less any inherited wealth, is what your net worth should be."

For example, if Mitch McKinney is forty-one years old and makes $150,000 a year, he would multiply $150,000 by forty-one. That comes to $6,150,000. Divide that amount by ten, and you find that Mitch's net worth should be $615,000 for him to be considered wealthy.

Most of us are not wealthy, but *becoming* wealthy is a great goal when we talk about our finances. Even if we don't reach the number suggested in the formula above, we will be much better off than if we don't have any goals at all. Increasing your cash flow and increasing your net worth should be priorities when constructing a successful financial plan.

I happened into a FedEx Kinko's in Toronto one day and started chatting with the copy clerk. I told her about this book, and she relayed her own story of wealth creation. Her name is Alina, and she is originally from China. She was a television journalist in her home country and, being in her late twenties, decided to come to Canada to seek more opportunity. She is making about $28,000 per year as a copy clerk. You may think, "She came all the way over here to be a copy clerk?" but not everything is what it seems.

Alina has more than $60,000 in assets invested in seven businesses in China. These businesses produce a monthly cash flow of $2,500 and are run by her sister. She is taking every bit of that money and reinvesting it to produce more cash flow. If all goes well, in five years she can retire from her copy clerk job (if she wants) and do whatever her heart desires—she won't even be thirty-five. She has more net worth as a copy clerk than most families have with professional incomes.

When it comes to our finances, what is meant by priorities? Priorities are the items that are important, rather than urgent. If you have a new baby in the household, then a priority would be to have an emergency fund. If you have teenagers about to attend college, then it's important that you have an education fund. If you are about to reach retirement age, then the amount you have set aside for your retirement is important.

Each person decides for himself what is important, because "important" will vary from person to person and will change depending on each person's situation. The trick is to make sure that you don't let the important items such as retirement get derailed by something that is urgent—for example, your children wanting a new home. The way to focus on the important priorities is to have goals and to have a plan.

When establishing priorities, it's important to include all stakeholders in the decision. Spouses certainly must be included. Children should be aware of the education fund that's established for them, and even contribute when possible. A household should establish its goals together so if sacrifices have to be made in lifestyle or luxuries, the meaning of those changes and the benefits that come from them are clear to everyone.

When considering financial planning and goal setting, it helps to begin with the end result in mind. Retirement planning should begin early in a young adult's life to give the magic of compounding a chance to take effect. Proper insurance should be purchased to protect the family financially in case of a disaster. These are basic financial principles that apply to everyone.

Before any thoughts of investing for the future can be considered, though, the monthly cash flow should be under control so that any money used for investments is healthy money—cash that is available for use after monthly bills are paid.

You may have questions about setting priorities. For example, *what if my priorities change?* A healthy person should have changing priorities throughout his life. He graduates college, gets married, has children, changes jobs, buys a house, gets ready to retire. Each of these situations requires a change in priorities. However, the key to handling a life change is to set up for it before the change occurs.

For example, if you are expecting a child, then you should have begun establishing an emergency fund long before the birth. Money should be saved for a down payment on a home, and as mentioned earlier, it's never too early to start saving for retirement. The problem with these ideas is that they require planning, and that is a learned skill.

Another question to ask yourself is *what do I have to work with*? Although a high income does not necessarily indicate wealth, a higher income *can* provide the tools to reach higher-level goals. One thing to consider, however, is whether your income is steady and whether it is flexible—that is, not already designated for a specific use.

Regardless of your situation, the goal should be to make progress financially. What is progress? Ultimately, financial progress is measured as an increase in your net worth. You increase your net worth by increasing your positive cash flow so you have something to work with. So increased cash flow would be considered progress.

An increase in the value of your investments and appreciable assets (those that go up in value) is a good sign of progress. According to Stanley and Danko, that's one of the ways millionaires do it.

Regardless of your particular goals, a few principles will keep you in good stead:

- **Pay yourself first. Make saving the first thing you do with your money.**

- **Set goals based on your priorities. Go with the important rather than the urgent.**

- **Give each dollar a purpose.**

- **Avoid impulse spending or buying.**

- **Structure your finances so you have a clear picture of where you are.**

More Money Than Month

CASH FLOW WORKSHEET

Monthly Income

Source	Dollar Amount
After-tax wages, bonuses	
Investment income, dividends	
Child support, alimony, any other maintenance income	
Miscellaneous income	
Total income	

Monthly Expenses

Category	Dollar Amount
Housing	
Rent or mortgage	
Utilities (heat, water, electric, phone, cable, etc.)	
Property taxes	
Homeowners insurance	
Miscellaneous housing fees	
Food	
Clothing	
Public transportation	
Car payment	
Auto insurance	

Registrations, licenses, fees	
Maintenance and gasoline	
Insurance (medical, life, etc.)	
Medical expenses	
Debts and loans	
Miscellaneous expenses	
Savings	
Total expenses	

Total monthly income	
− Total monthly expenses	
Total monthly cash flow	

NET WORTH WORKSHEET

Assets	Dollar Amount
Home	
Vehicles	
Bank accounts, cash on hand	
Investments, retirement accounts	
Insurance cash value	
Furniture, electronics, appliances	
Jewelry	
Collectibles	
Miscellaneous	
Total assets	

Liabilities	Dollar Amount
Home mortgage	
Car loans	
Revolving debt	
Other loans	
Miscellaneous	
Total liabilities	

Total assets	
− Total liabilities	
Total net worth	

Chapter 4

Connect the Dots

If you want to make progress, then you need to know two things—where you are and where you want to be. The previous chapter provided guidelines to help you clarify your current financial situation. This chapter will help you determine where you want to be and how to construct a workable plan to get there.

What exactly are your goals? A functional definition of a *goal* is a positive end result, established in advance, that you can achieve through your own efforts. The idea of a goal being positive should not be a surprise. Aiming for a *negative* end result is probably a sign of mental illness, which is beyond the scope of this book.

The end result is the image you have in your mind when you think about the new situation: a new car, a new home, financial security—the list can go on. It's important that you have a clear picture of the end result that you want to achieve. This gives your subconscious mind a target, so even if you are not consciously thinking about the goal, your subconscious mind is still working on it. Ideas will pop into your mind that you hadn't considered because of the clear information you gave your mind to work with.

Of course, the whole point of establishing a goal in advance is to be able to achieve it in the most efficient way possible. The end result might occur without planning, but that would merely be a series of fortunate events rather than a plan. It would probably also require a tremendous waste of resources to achieve. By establishing the goal in advance, you can connect the dots to get to it in the most cost-effective way possible.

A goal must also be something that you can achieve through your own efforts. "Winning the lottery," for example, would not be a goal because it relies on random chance. However, "establishing an emergency fund of enough money to cover three to six months of expenses" would be a great goal because you can accomplish it through your own actions.

There are two major points to this step. First, you must understand that *action* is required on your part if you are to reach your goal. If you only imagine something that you'd like to have, purchase, or be without any intention of taking the appropriate action to achieve it, then the mental picture is simply a dream or a wish. Goal setting is for people who recognize the real world for what it is—an environment that rewards action.

For anything to happen, creation must take place twice. The first creation must take place in the mind, when the image of the end result is formed, first nebulous and vague, then becoming clearer and more solid. The second creation is when you actually take action to complete the image and make it real. Without both creations, nothing is accomplished.

The second point is that you must be willing to pay the price to reach your goals. There is a saying that "if you keep doing what you've been doing, then you'll keep getting what you've been getting." If you are trying to achieve something that you haven't done before, then you will have to make changes in your mind-set and in your lifestyle. Some things in your life will have to be left behind. You might have to forgo that extra dinner out each week or that shopping trip every Saturday. Decide in advance that you will say no to these money drains, and then plan how you will handle your family's complaints. This is in their best interest, too, in the long run.

This is not as unpleasant as it may sound at first. You will be putting more important things—priorities—ahead of less important distractions. If you are trying to save money, then you may not be able to make that daily stop at the coffee shop—at least not every day. You may have to cut back on how often you buy yourself new clothes.

It's far better that you determine in advance what you are willing to sacrifice rather than have to give up other things by force. When you make changes to improve your life, you will pay a price, one way or another. If you consciously decide to do away with items that are not as important, you are deciding the price that you will pay. Some of the decisions will sting a little, but they will pay off in the long run, and the feeling of peace of mind is, as they say, priceless.

When Charles decided that he would build his nest egg no matter what, he didn't sabotage himself and give in to the desires of the moment—he was disciplined and took responsibility to make it happen. Sometimes this meant going without, but looking back at what he eventually accomplished, it wasn't that big of a sacrifice.

The goal-setting process does not have to be terribly complicated. You simply begin with the end result in mind, and then devise a series of smaller steps to reach that result. The steps can be as small or as large as you care to make them. Some of the steps may take you farther than you thought, enabling you to skip some of the later steps. The only thing that matters is that the first step should seem achievable from the perspective of your current situation.

At the beginning of the goal-setting process, don't worry too much about how you will achieve the end result. Part of the process is working out the steps to reach your goal, and if you try to figure it all out at the very beginning, you may feel as though the later steps are beyond your reach. So simply take a moment and evaluate your situation.

First, think about your current financial status. If you did your cash flow and net worth analyses, then you already know if you are in a relatively weak or relatively strong financial position. Like building a house, your financial structure must be built on a solid foundation and constructed from the ground up. You simply can't work on the top levels of your financial plan—investing in mutual funds, for example—until you have a positive cash flow. Having said that, investing in mutual funds would be a great goal—provided one of your first steps is to create positive cash flow.

When you analyzed your net worth, did you have more debt than you thought? Debt can definitely be a drag on building a successful financial future. Later in the book I will cover debt in more detail, but for now just realize that if you carry a lot of debt, especially on depreciating assets, then you are limiting your financial success.

Many people find it difficult to think about having goals when it comes to their finances. Of course, everyone wants more money, but few people have a step-by-step plan to obtain it. This process is the essence of goal setting. Setting goals has been proven time and again to help people achieve more than they ever thought possible.

Goal setting is the magic tool that helps people become and do more than they think they are capable of. When your mind is focused on a particular target, the target becomes clearer, and the subsequent objectives become easier to achieve. Those who are striving for particular goals are generally successful; those without goals are generally not.

The first step is to create an image of the end result. The more concrete and vivid your image of the goal is, the better. You are creating something real by first envisioning it in your mind. Every great accomplishment has first been conceived as a vision. Regardless of how varied the actual realization of the vision is, the inspiration was first.

On a more practical level, you don't start out on a trip and not have some sort of a plan in mind. If you are traveling cross-country to Grandma's house, you need to know where Grandma lives. You may take wrong turns along the way or stop and enjoy the sights, but ultimately you must know where you are headed.

When it comes to your financial situation, do you know where you want to be? At this point, think about some of your dreams and aspirations. How would having more money affect those dreams? Could you enjoy a better lifestyle with more financial security? Maybe you're thinking of a nice home or taking a pleasant vacation. Either of these can be a goal.

You may have more pragmatic goals, such as creating a positive cash flow. This goal is just as valid as any other, because it aims for improvement. Effective goals are those which show improvement in your life, instead of simply maintaining the status quo. Large or small, a goal that improves your life is the ideal.

A common danger that we face when we strive to improve our lives is the temptation to compare our goals with the goals of others. Each of us has individual characteristics, motivations, and abilities. If we are distracted by other people's goals or progress, we fool ourselves into believing that we are in a competition with those people. The truth is, we are only in competition with ourselves when we are working on self-improvement.

When deciding on your goals, consider the stage of life that you're currently in. If you are a young adult, fresh out of college, you will have very different goals from the married couple who turn sixty-five in two months. As a young adult, you may still be looking for your first job (at least the first "real" job) or considering getting married. You may be ready to start a family or buy your first home. This is the point where you would think long term and start your retirement fund.

As a middle-aged adult, you are probably settled into your career—although a career change is always possible and would affect your plans. You may have children or even grandchildren for whom you want to establish an education fund. You may begin experiencing health issues that would affect your goals.

As you mature, your temperament and outlook may change. What made you impatient when you were younger may no longer affect you the same way. Unexpected events—divorce, physical accidents, separation from a job—may make certain goals more appealing than they were previously and other goals less appealing.

If you are a senior, you may be thinking about retirement—or not. Many seniors are working longer and enjoying their lives at a level of activity that would have shocked seniors fifty years ago. Your home may be paid off, and your health may be a major factor in your decision making. The idea of retirement is undergoing a bit of a revolution. People no longer plan to quit work and sit on the porch in a rocking chair for the rest of their lives. They travel and really live!

Many boomers are starting to engage in what is known as *creative retirement*, in which they work at least part time but often not in the industry that their career was in. I know a man who was a banker and now teaches scuba diving part time. He travels to the Caribbean one week each month to take groups of scuba enthusiasts on the trip of a lifetime. I know another man in his early sixties who is a real estate agent part time, though he retired as a paramedic. He has learned to invest in real estate and now has more cash flow than when he was working full time. These types of activities affect the money you will need at retirement, and financial advisers are struggling to take these types of creative living into account when helping clients plan for the future.

The three stages of life are arbitrary, and different people will have the same goals at different points in their lives. Some people marry young, while others marry later in life or repeatedly. The stages are not designed to define or pigeonhole someone regarding her age, but are used to refer to the separate phases that our lives are naturally divided into.

In all of these cases, your stage of life and the particular situation you find yourself in determine your goals. Look at the needs you face at the moment and the ones you will face in the near future. Goals will often overlap, and planning ahead is important. It's also never too soon to start preparing for your needs in the distant future, sometimes so far ahead you can barely see the goal. By planning far ahead, however, you take advantage of the power of compounding. In general, though, there are stage-appropriate goals.

Financial goals can generally be classified in three ways—short term, intermediate, and long term. Short-term goals usually involve smaller dollar amounts and a shorter amount of time. A good definition of a short-term financial goal is one that can realistically be reached in less than one or two years.

Some examples of short-term goals are buying a new car, going on vacation, and saving for Christmas. Other goals might be to create a positive cash flow, to establish an emergency fund, or to become debt free (this may take a bit longer depending on the amount of debt you have).

After you've determined your goal, it's time to break it down into steps. Because a short-term goal involves less time, there will likely be fewer steps than for a goal with a longer time horizon. For example, if you decide you want to create a positive cash flow, you may (1) increase your income by taking a second job; (2) decrease expenses by paying off and decreasing your use of credit cards; (3) trade in your vehicle for one that's more fuel efficient and less expensive.

You could reduce the steps further if you wanted to. For example, in "taking a second job," you might list steps like this: (1) Decide what skills and talents you have that you could use to earn extra income. (2) Search the phone book to find companies that could pay you for your skills or talent. (3) Determine which of those companies appeals to you. One may be closer to your home, or another might be in an industry that you enjoy. (4) Contact those companies and ask if they are hiring part-time help. (5) Go to the company and apply for a job.

This is a very simplistic example, of course, but it shows some of the steps you could take to create a positive cash flow. If you wanted, you could go into more detail about what kind of job you are going to get, how many hours you need to work, etc. Personalize your process as much as you need to so each step feels like something you can accomplish. (Goal worksheets are included at the end of this chapter to assist you.)

Intermediate goals are those that generally take three to ten years to achieve. You might start some of these while you are still working on your short-term goals; overlap is okay as long as it doesn't interfere with your overall financial health. Don't remove money from your emergency fund to invest in the stock market, for example.

Some examples of intermediate goals are to put a down payment on a home or to begin investing. You might incorporate some of your short-term goals to achieve your intermediate goals. For example, creating a positive cash flow could help you get out of debt. Getting out of debt gives you more money to use as a down payment or to invest.

Long-term goals are those that generally take more than ten years to accomplish. With these goals, the magic of compound interest and time work in your favor. Retirement funds, for instance, are often at the end of a thirty- or forty-year program. A young couple might start a college fund for their baby, giving them eighteen years to build it.

Because they have the weight of years of preparation behind them, long-term goals have a lot more importance. For example, your retirement fund is what you will live on if you are no longer able to work and earn money for yourself, or if you choose to retire and live a particular lifestyle. Money devoted to your retirement should be invested according to your personal risk tolerance and time horizon, and not removed without a very good reason.

There is a definite process for goal setting. Although the following characteristics and steps are intended for use in your financial success, they can be used in any area of your life that you want to improve. As I mentioned at the beginning of the chapter, goal setting is a process, and as long as it works, whatever method you use is fine. You can begin with the process outlined below and adapt it as you want. It can be tailored to every type of goal, so use it and tinker with it until it works perfectly for your individual goals.

When determining your goal, the first step is to make sure that your goal is *specific*. You need to create a picture in your mind that is as concrete and vivid as possible. If you want to achieve a positive cash flow, then imagine your balance sheet that shows much more income than expenses. If you want a new car, what kind of car is it? Do you want a sedan, a convertible, or perhaps a hybrid?

You need to be specific because you want to put your subconscious mind to work. The subconscious mind is the boss of the conscious mind. You decide things for reasons you're not clear on, but the subconscious mind has definite plans. By creating a vivid image, you are removing unnecessary distractions so your mind has a chance to focus on the goal.

Your goal should have a *time frame*. If you set your goal without any deadline, you lose the sense of urgency it takes to accomplish anything. For example, you might say, "Within three years, I will have an emergency fund of three to six months' worth of expenses." This goal provides a time frame for the goal to be accomplished. You now know how long you have to complete the goal, and you can break it down into appropriate smaller steps.

Let's say that your goal for the emergency fund is $10,000. If you divide $10,000 by three years, you see that you must save $3,333.33 a year, or $277.78 a month. Without having a specific timeline, you wouldn't know how much you needed to save each month.

Remember, your goal should be *achievable*, something that you can do as a result of your own efforts. One of the dangers here is to limit your ambitions, because when you look at your goal, it seems as though it's not achievable. If you find something that you really want, take a moment to see if you can break it down into smaller elements that are not as intimidating.

When you find yourself looking at a big goal that seems beyond your reach, try thinking to yourself, "If I were the kind of person who could do this, what would I do?" Sometimes you can shake loose the doubt by stepping back and looking at the situation more objectively. You will often find that the answer is there, and simply by completing a series of incremental steps, you can accomplish the goal you want.

Another characteristic of your goal is that it must be *measurable*. For instance, in the example about the emergency fund, the goal would be better stated, "I will have an emergency fund of $10,000 within three years." This is a better statement of the goal because it is simple to know when you have $10,000 in your account, but saying "three to six months' worth of expenses" is less defined, so it's hard to know exactly when you reach it.

If your goal is not measurable, how will you know when you've reached it? A vague goal will do one of two things: it will frustrate you because you don't ever seem to reach a successful conclusion, or you will claim victory even though the improvement is not what you were really hoping for. In either case, self-deception is working against you.

Finally, a goal must be *ethical.* You must strive for goals that do not violate your personal sense of right and wrong. We work for goals to improve ourselves, and in so doing benefit society as a whole. Purposely working for a goal that you know is unethical or immoral (not to mention illegal) will create a mental and emotional conflict that will sabotage your efforts.

If you choose worthy goals and create a process using the previous steps, your success will be that much closer to coming true. Without goals and planning, your chances for success are diminished. Although it seems to be almost a magical tool, goal setting simply puts the power of your will, discipline, and energy to work for your improvement. Remember the definition of a goal at the beginning of the chapter: a positive end result, established in advance, that you can achieve through your own efforts.

Todd Dean

FINANCIAL GOAL-SETTING WORKSHEET

Goals	Dollar Amount Needed	Number of Months until Needed	Dollar Amount to Be Saved Each Month
Short term (< three years)			
Intermediate (three to ten years)			
Long term (> ten years)			

Chapter 5
Digging Out of the Pit

shopaholic [shop-a-<u>hol</u>-ic]: a compulsive shopper who suffers from uncontrolled overspending

I have mentioned debt quite a bit throughout the book, and it's clear that debt is a powerful force to be dealt with. But the truth is, debt is not the cause of all the financial problems I've outlined, but merely a symptom. Debt does not occur spontaneously by itself—it is created through choice.

Of course, debt is helpful in some ways. Families can buy a home without having to pay cash. They can put their money to use building equity in a property that they own instead of spending it on rent.

Other forms of debt unfortunately can act as an anchor that prevents us from realizing our dreams. We buy something on credit, infatuated with it at the moment, then the glow wears off, and all that's left are the payments. What should be a source of pleasure is instead nothing but a series of payments that sometimes goes years into the future. Those who display all of their possessions as a badge of honor sometimes face bad credit, no cash, and even repossession or bankruptcy.

Historically, America has not been a country of debtors. Until about one hundred years ago, items were bought with cash, or goods were traded. Businesses occasionally paid with checks. According to a paper from the Federal Reserve Bank in Philadelphia, it was in the early 1900s that companies first issued proprietary credit cards, accepted only at that company's stores. Any balances charged were paid the next month.

In 1950, Diners Club issued the first multicompany card that could be used for travel and entertainment at different businesses that accepted the card. In 1966, Bank of America issued the prototype card that is in general use now and is accepted at countless locations around the world.

The marketing of credit cards in the last four decades has been unbelievably successful. In 1970, only 16 percent of households had a credit card, but by 1995, 65 percent had at least one credit card. During that time, consumer credit began its upward climb. The Federal Reserve reported that

More Money Than Month

in May 2008, Americans had $961.8 billion in revolving credit, 98 percent in the form of credit cards.

Clearly Shakespeare's dictum of "neither a borrower nor a lender be" was long ago discarded. America's own philosopher Benjamin Franklin said, "He that goes a-borrowing goes a-sorrowing." With the number of Americans who have recently found themselves in financial trouble—sometimes to the point of bankruptcy—Franklin's words ring truer than ever. As a society, modern culture indulges in debt to a degree that our grandparents would not recognize.

This is not to say that debt cannot be a useful tool. There are always emergencies in which using a credit card is the only way to save the day. Car repairs, emergency room visits, and other times when we are at our wit's end seem like good times to use the credit card. More often, however, we loosely define the word "emergency" until we use the card whenever it's inconvenient to get cash.

Credit cards are also often used when families need to buy food and they are short of cash. They hope they will have the funds when the credit card bill comes due. Unfortunately for a large number of families, using the credit card only makes matters worse, sinking them deeper in debt. They wind up unable to pay the balance when it is due, so instead they pay the minimum payment—thereby financing impulsive or short-term purchases for months or years.

Credit—usually in the form of credit cards—can provide luxuries for those to whom such things are important. Many people enjoy the status of having the newest fashions, the biggest television, or the latest electronic gadget, even if they have to pay with credit. These consumers are trying to display the trappings of wealth without having the money to back it up.

Oftentimes credit cards are used during the holidays when parents who are suffering financial trouble vow that their children will still have a good Christmas. These parents are trying to give the impression of financial security when there is anything but. They underestimate the ability of the children to detect tension in the air and the strength of their children, who may be satisfied with fewer gifts if it means their parents will be more relaxed.

Then there are those who suffer a genuine malady that can only be soothed by spending. The shopaholic who comes home with shopping bags full of items paid for with credit cards is the stereotype. With the advent of television shopping networks and the ease of shopping on the Internet, spending has never been easier.

Those individuals who have an emotional need to shop can sate their appetites, at least temporarily, by using credit. The downside of this particular "benefit" is that often the shopaholic is overcome with guilt after the purchase when she realizes the financial damage that she may have caused herself or her family.

The negatives of debt and the use of credit far outweigh the benefits in today's society. The easy availability of credit creates in consumers a hunger for, even an expectation of, products that are outside their financial reach. When anything is advertised, our eye is immediately drawn to it. If a new car rolls down the street, we imagine ourselves in the driver's seat.

The hunger has become so strong that we are willing to sacrifice more important items in order to possess the trifle that most recently caught our attention. We would know that almost all of these items are beyond our reach if we simply sat down and did the math. We may be able to create a plan to purchase these items at some point in the future, but easy credit has made such waiting unnecessary, so we purchase them anyway, not realizing the full cost of that easy credit.

Such easy availability of credit also leads to poor spending habits. Credit cards are issued to consumers who don't have the discipline to control their spending. They use the credit card, and it is as if they are spending Monopoly money. They stop being choosy shoppers, and the need for satisfaction causes them to purchase items that they normally wouldn't if they were paying with cash.

Studies show that shoppers who pay with credit cards spend an average of 12 to 18 percent more than when they pay with cash. One reason is ease of use; you hand the cashier your card, sign, and you're on your way. Parting with cash causes pain. Cash is a tangible representation of the fruits of our labors, and it is psychologically harder to separate from cash. When we use credit, we bypass all the pain—or at least postpone it.

Debt also converts pleasure to pain. As I mentioned earlier, the car payments last a long time after the new-car smell is gone. Many times families suffer because their car payment is so large that it impacts their quality of life. What once brought them joy is now bringing down everything else in their life.

A pattern of credit abuse, late payments, disconnections, and possibly even repossession can destroy a family's credit rating. With a low credit score, anything they charge will likely be at a higher interest rate, and the economic spiral winds down, getting worse and worse. The appetite to buy has caused many families to face financial ruin.

As destructive as debt can be, even financially responsible people find one type of debt necessary—the home mortgage. According to the U.S. Census Bureau, the median price for a home in May 2008 was $231,000, an amount well beyond the ability of most families to be able to save for in advance. Arranging a mortgage lets the consumer begin building a solid financial future.

Most financial experts agree that owning your own home is one of the cornerstones of a successful economic plan. Homes are investments because they appreciate in value over time. As you make mortgage payments, you build equity in the home, creating a larger net worth. For most homeowners, the home is the largest asset and the biggest source of net worth. Timely payments increase the equity and improve the credit score.

Even considering a mortgage as a necessary debt, however, does not mean that most traditional mortgages can't be improved. Choosing a fifteen-year, rather than a thirty-year, mortgage can cut thousands of dollars off the total cost of buying the home. Adding extra amounts to the scheduled payment increases the equity and pays off the mortgage faster.

In fact, if a family were able to eliminate all other debt and concentrate on paying off the mortgage early, they could save thousands of dollars and years of payments. A family with no debt whatsoever is in a tremendous position to build wealth. Even with a necessary debt such as a mortgage, it is advantageous to eliminate it as quickly as possible.

This is not to say that a mortgage is for everyone or every situation. There are times—such as when you know you will be in one location for less than two years, when you decide to get out from under a large mortgage, if you might lose your job, or when your spouse dies—that renting is a good solution. After you know your location and situation is going to be somewhat stable for more than three years, then a mortgage might make sense. But each situation must be evaluated individually.

The unnecessary debt that the majority of us carry, on the other hand, has no redeeming features as far as financial health. Easy credit offers quick satisfaction of the spending urge but little else. Credit cards encourage you to spend more than you have the ability to pay, tempting consumers to overextend themselves and fall deeper into debt.

Bank cards such as Visa and MasterCard are accepted almost everywhere, which can lead their cardholders to use credit to pay for fast-food meals and other consumables that should rightly be paid with cash. Although some customers pay their balance each month, the amount of debt that Americans carry shows that the vast majority are financing their lifestyles at the expense of their future.

Some credit cards are *proprietary*, meaning they can only be used at one store or with one company. A furniture store, for example, may issue a credit card that can be used to furnish a home. Home improvement stores, department stores, jewelry stores—they all profit by making it easier for their customers to spend money with them. The credit business grows until a company that purports to sell goods actually makes a large part of its profit from credit and financing.

More Money Than Month

Those people who find themselves strapped for cash become customers of companies that grant *payday loans*—short-term loans for those who are in a financial bind and are to be paid back with their next paycheck. With fees, the interest rate on these loans can reach almost 400 percent. With all the extra charges, borrowers often are unable to make it through another pay period without help, so they roll the loan over to be paid with the next paycheck … and the finance charges keep growing.

The U.S. government is involved in debt on a large scale, of course. As of this writing, the national debt is over $9 trillion. Various economists have theories about the dangers of the government carrying this much debt, but the main point is that we have grown used to seeing and hearing about debt on a very large scale. In fact, we have become so used to being exposed to debt that the idea of carrying a large debt no longer shocks us. What shocks us anymore is the idea of having *no* debt.

When it comes to debt, "large-scale" is a relative term. For a family, a $400,000 mortgage may seem huge (depending on your location). Financing a $30,000 car may be intimidating. As a percentage of our debt, shelter and transportation are usually the largest portions of our debt burden. The numbers of the government's debt are too large for most of us to even comprehend.

Without going into an extensive analysis of the effects of the government deficit on the economy, we can look at one factor. First of all, money is a commodity, just like wheat or pork bellies. When the government borrows money, it borrows just like any of the rest of us, from the common pool of lenders. In other words, the government increases the *demand* for money.

When there is a larger demand for a commodity, the price goes up. The "price" on money is what we call the interest rate. As the government borrows more and more money, the markets are pressured to increase the interest rates that all of us pay. This in turn affects credit cards, home mortgages, auto loans, and any other product that charges interest.

Like a line of dominoes, many other parts of the economy—unemployment, new-home sales, manufacturing, etc.—are affected by the government's debt. These issues also affect our families as we try to make ends meet among the various financial pressures that can control our lives if we let them.

The increased pressure causes more stress, worry, and anxiety because we have positioned ourselves so delicately. Often a single bad turn in the economy can create turmoil in the household finances. When we carry a huge debt load in our own household, we are more vulnerable to the fluctuations of the national economy.

In this extensive explanation of the perils of debt, it pays to go back and read the message at the very beginning of the chapter—debt is not the enemy, it is a symptom. The real enemy is the lack of financial discipline that most of us display occasionally and that some of us display chronically. Unfortunately, a number of forces seek to exploit that all-too-human weakness.

First of all, companies that offer credit are part of the problem. Even the ones that have good intentions have to compete for consumer dollars and often become very aggressive. The worst of the credit companies use deceptive practices, everything from predatory clauses in the fine print to outright fraud.

All of them use aggressive marketing aimed at the most vulnerable consumers. Nearly all college students begin to receive credit card applications before they get through their freshman year. The constant financial struggle that most college students face makes them particularly susceptible to easy credit.

Credit card applications have been sent to children, dead people, and even pets. The credit industry is indiscriminate in who it markets to for credit. In recent years, public advocacy groups have put pressure on the government to regulate some of the more heinous practices of the credit card industry, but it is still up to the individual to refuse to be victimized by some of the tactics of the credit card companies.

More Money Than Month

One of the more reprehensible areas of behavior used by credit card companies is their collection practices. Technically, most of them are within legal guidelines in how they try to collect money owed to them. However, the collection agents are masters at inspiring fear in the customer regarding possible consequences of late payments, to the extent that many people pay their credit card balance before they pay their mortgage.

When I talk about priorities, this is one of the areas where establishing priorities is most pertinent. Most people, when in a rational state of mind, would agree that it is more important to make the house payment before paying a credit card bill. Unfortunately, the collection agents can cause the customer to become emotionally upset, and rational thought is left behind. The decision to pay a secondary item like a credit card—even though the agent is justified and the debt should be paid—before paying a primary debt like the mortgage would not be made under normal circumstances.

Besides the marketers, another enemy to our financial health is advertising. Advertising agencies employ psychology in masterful ways to entice customers to want their clients' products. In advertising, beer drinkers are always having a fun time and are surrounded by friends. Coffee is sipped in a beautiful home at a beautiful breakfast table by beautiful people. A pair of sneakers can make you jump higher or run faster.

Consumers don't consciously believe these concepts, and if you asked them, they would likely realize how artificial the circumstances in advertisements are. Commercials are aired during television programs while we are in a relaxed state of mind and more receptive to unspoken messages such as those used by advertisers.

Advertisers create a hunger for products in the public. With billions of dollars of debt hanging over our heads, that hunger should be satisfied. Yet the spending continues, with customers using debt to finance their purchases, even as advertisers come up with new ways to sell us new products that we have no business wanting.

Marketers and advertisers are doing their jobs. In a capitalist, free-enterprise society, consumers should be made aware of products that are available to them. However, each of us must understand the expertise and the vast quantity of resources that are being used to sell us items to the detriment of our finances. If we understand how companies are manipulating our emotions, we also realize we hold the supremely powerful option of simply saying *no*.

Companies are not the only enemy when it comes to our maintaining our financial equilibrium. The media does its part to convince us that what we see on television, in the movies, and in magazines is what our expectations should be. By showing so-called middle-class characters who don't face the financial burdens that real people face, television creates the impression that our own problems are unusual, that we should be able to live like those characters on television.

This constant attention on high-level lifestyles is not necessarily the *fault* of the media. However, the *consequences* of the images they broadcast into our homes are devastating. The psychological pressure on consumers to upgrade their lifestyles is almost irresistible. To the detriment of society, we have lost much of the willpower it takes to sacrifice lower-priority luxuries for higher-priority necessities. The avalanche of temptation offered by the media does not help.

As adults, much of our purchasing behavior and buying patterns would seem to be under our own control. In truth, much of our behavior—not just in purchasing, but throughout our lives—is influenced by other people. Our parents have the largest effect, of course, because of the nature of our relationships with our families.

Parents have an unassailable authority in all that they do in connection with their children. Everything parents do is the way it ought to be done, even if the evidence indicates otherwise. If our parents believed it was important to purchase large items on credit, then we probably grew up with that same belief. Even if we resist what we realize are bad behaviors, subconsciously we still compare ourselves to our parents when we conduct our own affairs.

More Money Than Month

Parents also have a major influence because of the volume of interactions they have with their children. Every spoken word, every action, every gesture or look conveys a message to a child. If a child expresses a desire to buy a particular item, a cocked eyebrow can make him question his choice. Parental disapproval may influence that child's choices for the rest of his life.

As adults we still follow the programming we were taught as children, unless we have managed to reprogram ourselves. Comparisons to our parents may direct us to drive a particular car, frequent a particular store, or handle our money a particular way. Spendthrift parents often raise children who become spendthrift adults. Unfortunately, we are now a few generations distant from the first group of citizen to be influenced by television and mass marketing. The effects seem to grow from one generation to the next.

Our financial habits are also greatly influenced by our peers. If we feel that we must belong to a particular group, we do everything we can to blend in and not stand out. If that group dresses a certain way, we also want to dress that way. This behavior is not restricted to schoolchildren; think of the number of women who have been told that a particular hairstyle is "too young" for her, or the men who feel they must wear the colors of the local sports team.

Many times these attempts at conformity come at a cost. Families that live in a neighborhood are expected to live a certain lifestyle, including the cars they drive, their home furnishings, and often the clubs and organizations they belong to. If a family has purchased a house that is too expensive for their income, they will struggle to accommodate the tastes and expectations of their neighbors and peers.

Such habits can derail the best of financial plans. Money spent on consumables or depreciating assets (such as vehicles and home furnishings) is unavailable for debt reduction or investing toward the future. Often consumers are upside down on their depreciating assets, resulting in a *negative* net worth. For those who aspire to increase their wealth, such behavior is dysfunctional and destructive.

Compulsive shopping can be considered an *addiction*, in that the compulsive shopper receives a high from shopping and will seek it at the expense of more important necessities. The compulsion to shop overrides practical concerns and often leads to financial self-destruction. The shopping often is used to replace something that is lacking in the person's life.

A recent *Washington Post* article reports that more than ten million people may be classified as shopaholics, people whose desire to shop, spend, and buy outweighs all practical considerations. The article reports that the American Psychiatric Association is considering whether to classify compulsive buying as a disorder.

Our spending habits are not restricted to big-ticket items, such as automobiles and jewelry. Many of us bleed financially with multiple small purchases every day—the cup of gourmet coffee every morning (or more often), multiple trips to the snack machine at work or school, the ever more expensive habit of smoking.

If you spend $4 for a cup of gourmet coffee every morning five days a week, that adds up to about $1,000 a year. Two $1 trips to the snack machine a day add up to another $500 a year. A pack-a-day cigarette habit costs you, conservatively speaking, about $2,000 a year. That's $3,500 a year that could go to reducing debt or making investments.

Although it's not easy, we can change our spending habits. We must learn to find fulfillment in the permanent, healthy habit of growing our wealth. This fulfillment can replace the temporary, unhealthy high we get from thoughtless spending. By concentrating on the pleasure we derive from providing for our family's well-being or on our preparations for a prosperous future, we can overcome the imagined loss of status or fulfillment from poor spending habits.

By eliminating poor money choices, we can change our entire lifestyle. Instead of worrying about being able to pay bills, trying to keep up with the Joneses, or suffering anxiety over the least financial misfortune, we can concentrate on living a lifestyle in which we can enjoy our relationships.

More Money Than Month

We can take pride in the freedom we will experience by living as debt free as possible. We can celebrate every increase in our net worth. We can enjoy the uniqueness that separates us from the mass of consumers whose actions are dictated by the media, predatory lenders, and marketers. We can look at those who are hopelessly in debt and feel sympathy for their plight because we, too, once lived that way.

The first steps to financial independence are the most difficult. It takes enormous intensity and dedication to separate ourselves from early programming and from the social pressures that force us to make poor financial decisions. At times we may feel hopeless when we do without those luxury items that everyone around us seems to have.

The struggle will be easier if we keep the end in mind, because living well is much more satisfying if the few extravagances we enjoy are paid for in themselves without sacrificing more important items. When we exert our willpower and self-control, we may feel as though we are living in a way that other people are not. At the end of the struggle, however, we will enjoy our financial freedom in a way that other people *cannot*.

Now before you get too depressed by the debt that may be surrounding you, let's also look at the other side of the equation: more income. One of the best ways to ease your current debt woes and create additional income for investing is by creating multiple streams of income (MSIs). It is no secret that by starting a business of your own that you can take advantage of all the tax breaks and deductions offered only to businesspeople. You can also associate with other businesspeople who can give you more ideas and even more opportunities to make even more money.

The best way to describe a great MSI is to explain what it is not. It is not another job. The perfect MSI make money for you without your active involvement once they get going. There is only one of you and only so many hours in the day; you can only be one place at a time. So you need to leverage yourself and think of ways to create more income and more passive income.

One of the fun activities that I do in my seminars is to take a group of people who can't see how they will make more money and create a mastermind group. A *mastermind group* is a group of people who are likeminded and have some of the same goals you have. They all get together and brainstorm solutions to each other's problems, which creates ideas that you may have never even thought to try.

I took one group and had them brainstorm two different situations. The first was for a retired couple. He is a retired maintenance supervisor at a local college, and she is a retired schoolteacher. How many different businesses could this couple start?

Here's what the group came up with:

1. Dog sitting/dog taxi

2. General handyman

3. Selling products on eBay

4. Build furniture/birdhouses

5. Senior taxi

6. Personal shopping with home delivery

7. Fencing contractor

These ideas were really pretty good! Never think that you don't have something to offer because of your age or work status. There are always ways to produce income if you choose to, and just because you set up the business doesn't mean you do all the work. You can always hire other retirees who want to get out and earn a little extra on the side.

More Money Than Month

The second scenario the group brainstormed was for a single mom, age thirty-two. I chose this scenario because most people have it considerably easier than a single mom, but this goes to show that you can still make some extra cash if you so choose.

The list the group came up with follows:

1. Day care or after-school program

2. Weekend childcare

3. Carpool for other moms

4. Ready-made meals

5. Tutor

6. Premade mixes (baking, etc.)

7. Children's parties

A sitter isn't needed in most of these situations, and they can be done mostly from home. This goes to show that a little creativity is all you need to enhance both sides of your financial equation. It is also evidence of the power of a mastermind group to help you see options and possibilities that you aren't aware of right now.

Chapter 6
Credit and Interest

Almost everyone knows they have a credit score, but not everyone knows how lenders arrive at that number or how it impacts their overall finances, including their ability to reach their financial goals. Credit scores originated as a quick way for lenders to assess someone's risk of default on a loan. Lenders, by their nature, are risk adverse, and they needed a consistent way to determine whom to lend to and what interest rate they deserve based on their credit worthiness.

Maintaining a good credit score allows you to receive lower interest rates for things like mortgages and other loans. Companies also sometimes use credit scores to determine if you will receive insurance coverage or be hired for a particular job. Not knowing how credit scores work or what you can do to improve them can harm you significantly over the long haul.

For example, if your score is considered less than great, it could cost you an extra 2 percent on your mortgage. Although that doesn't sound like much, if a particular mortgage is $250,000 and someone with good credit gets a rate of 6.25 percent for 30 years and someone with some past credit problems gets a rate of 8.25 percent, the person with worse credit will pay an additional $121,987.89 over the life of the loan due to a mere 2 percent difference in the rate. If you had a past bankruptcy or some very serious credit problems, you might pay 9.25 percent in this situation, and your additional interest compared to the 6.25 percent rate would be a whopping $186,257.75! This is a result of the cumulative effect of compound interest on the money you borrowed at the additional 3 percent over the life of the loan, which is 30 years. Just as compound interest can work for you over the long haul with investments, it can also work against you in the form of interest payments if you have poor credit.

The FICO scoring system, developed by a company named Fair Isaac Corp., is the most common scoring system. Though the numbers generated by this system can impact your financial well-being for years, the way you are scored is still largely a secret. Companies claim that the formulas are proprietary and that if you and I knew too much about them, we'd be able to play the system and raise our scores.

Due to this secrecy, myths and rumors abound as to what really helps your score and what doesn't. Although mortgage brokers and lenders may think they are helping when they tell you to close credit accounts that you don't use, they are really harming your score and your future ability to get credit.

In 2007 Fair Isaac Corp. announced that it was developing a new scoring model that would affect credit scores as early as 2008. The new system gives lenders a better idea of those who might default because they have been negatively impacted by the mortgage and credit crisis. What this means for you is that if you have an occasional late payment or slipup, the scoring system will not weight those as heavily as it will the consistently late payments from the repeat offender.

The FICO score, which Fair Isaac says is used by 90 percent of the one hundred largest banks, and other similar credit scores have a large impact on consumers. The latest version of the FICO score will largely look and feel the same to consumers and lenders. Scores will still range from 300 to 850—the higher the better—and the model will continue to determine scores based on the same factors, including consumers' overall percentage of debt and payment histories, length of credit histories, number of recent credit openings and inquiries, and the type of credit used.

Despite the new scoring model, you still have to make sure the information in your credit report, which Fair Isaac relies on to come up with its score, is accurate. If you feel your FICO score is unfair, you have to get a copy of your credit report from each credit bureau (Experian Group Ltd., TransUnion LLC, and Equifax Inc.) and look for any errors or missing information. If there are any, you have to contact the credit bureau or the financial institutions to dispute those errors.

The average person doesn't realize how important her score is until she suffers a major financial catastrophe, such as an accident or illness, loss of a job, or even divorce. Although it can take years to build a good credit score, that score can be devastated in mere months if you are unaware.

Though few people give much thought to their actual scores, lenders do—and that translates into the interest rates you are offered when you apply for credit. When you think about your mortgage, car loans, credit cards, and other forms of debt, you can imagine that a few points' difference in interest can add up to thousands, or even tens or hundreds of thousands of dollars over time. But it's not just the money.

The insurance industry often uses credit scores as a basis to not only raise customers' rates, but also to deny insurance to some. Though insurers commonly claim a strong link between a person's credit score and his insurance risk, no study to date has shown more than a casual link between the two. Not only can your credit score impact your ability to get a loan, it can open you up to increased insurance premiums or increased risk if you are denied insurance.

Credit Repair

If you have had some problems paying your bills on time, you can do several things to help lessen the impact and repair the problem. First, realize that you are not alone. Millions of people in the U.S. and Canada have credit problems severe enough to make getting a loan with decent terms very difficult. Even if you would consider your credit fair or average, you may want to improve it—especially if you know you will be making a major purchase in the near future, such as buying a home.

New knowledge of how credit scores are created allows people to improve their score and also reveals how wrong many financial gurus have been when giving advice on improving scores.

According to a recent survey of major lenders, though credit scores range from 300 to 850, only about 11 percent of the population ranks above 800 and is considered to have stellar credit. Those with very good credit rank between 750 and 799 and comprise about 29 percent of the population. This means that 61 percent of the population falls into the good, fair, or poor credit categories. If you are one of these, you can take several steps to improve your score and get the best interest rates possible.

More Money Than Month

First, pay on time. Calculations allocate 35 percent of your total credit score to this one area, for good reason. If a lender wants to know if you are a good risk, then paying bills on time is a very strong indicator. It is important to note that in credit scores, recent history is much more heavily weighted, which means you can have a significant impact on your credit score in a short period of time. By the same token, late payments can devastate your score. Missing even one payment can knock 50 to 100 points off a good score. If you know you have trouble remembering which bill to pay on what date, then a good path for you may be to automate as many of the payments as possible.

Next, lower your percentage of revolving debt. Lenders like the look of a responsible attitude when it comes to how much debt you carry on a continual basis. Having credit cards constantly charged to the max is not a good sign in their eyes. Your best course of action is to pay down your debt below 30 percent of available credit on all your credit cards and charge less. Your credit score doesn't distinguish between those who carry a balance on their cards and those who don't. So charging less or carrying a zero balance actually improves your score because it shows a higher percentage of available credit. However, for years financial people advised those trying to improve their score to close unused accounts, and this actually hurts your score! Knowing that the percentage of debt is a factor in your score allows you to pay down your credit cards to improve your score if you know you will soon be applying for a car loan or mortgage.

This information can be frustrating to those who want to simplify their lives and reduce the opportunities for identity theft by closing unused accounts. But this is how the numbers are calculated, and it is in your best interest to know. Closing credit accounts lowers the total credit available to you and makes any balances you have loom larger in credit score calculations. If you close your oldest accounts, it can actually shorten the length of your reported credit history and make you seem less creditworthy. However, if you don't use your cards much and your score is already high, the damage caused by closing more recent unused accounts will be minimal and may be well worth the peace of mind. If you do carry balances or charge frequently, leave all of your old accounts open, especially if you're about to apply for new credit.

Don't take every offer to apply for a credit card—even if the store clerk offers you a big discount on your purchases. Each new application lowers your score a bit and, more important, offers a chance for identity thieves to get your information, especially if you are filling out forms in a department store that can be accessed by anyone. It is much better to apply only for credit accounts that you really need and to manage them wisely.

The Magic of Compounding

In the world of investing, compounding is everything. It makes your lonely little dollar accumulate over time into hundreds of dollars all on its own. Most people have a pretty good understanding of what interest is, but there are two types: simple and compound. An example of simple interest would be if you have $100,000 in your account and get 6 percent interest, you receive $6,000. The next year, and every year after that, you would also receive $6,000 on the principal of $100,000. After ten years, you have a total of $160,000: the $100,000 in principal and the $6,000 received each year for ten years.

With compound interest, the $6,000 you receive the first year would be added to the original balance. The next year you would receive not only the $6,000 in interest on the original $100,000, but an additional $360 on the $6,000 in interest received the year before. Receiving interest on your interest is called *compounding* and looks something like this:

	Account Balance	Interest
Year 1	$100,000.00	$6,000.00
Year 2	$106,000.00	$6,360.00
Year 3	$112,360.00	$6,741.60
Year 4	$119,101.60	$7,146.10
Year 5	$126,247.70	$7,574.86
Year 6	$133,822.56	$8,029.35
Year 7	$141,851.91	$8,511.11

Year 8	$150,363.03	$9,021.78
Year 9	$159,384.81	$9,563.09
Year 10	$168,947.90	$10,136.87
Total	$179,084.77	

Rather than just ending up with $160,000 in your account as you would with simple interest, you have $179,084.77 with no effort whatsoever on your part! The most important thing to understand about money is its relationship to time. You can see the difference if I take this same example and project it out thirty years. With simple interest you would have a total of $280,000—sounds pretty nice doesn't it? But look at what happens to the compound interest over thirty years:

	Account Balance	Interest
Year 1	$100,000.00	$6,000.00
Year 10	$179,084.77	$10,745.09
Year 20	$320,713.55	$19,242.81
Year 30	$574,349.12	$34,460.95
Total	$608,810.06	

The total is a whopping $608,810! Now you can see why people call this the "magic" of compounding. The difference in this example between compound interest and simple interest is $328,810, which is a big difference if you're trying to live the life you want. The more time you give your investments, the more you increase the income potential of your original principal, which takes the pressure off of you to have to make every single dollar. Let your money work for you instead of sitting around doing nothing.

When you think of investing, it is very important not to attach a calendar-year mentality. You are looking for an average, which allows you to compare the lows versus the highs. Doing this injects some objectivity into your perspective, and you will see that a bad year is not as devastating as it may feel.

You may also want to compare your credit card costs to your market returns. If you are earning 8 percent in the market and obsess over it but carry credit card debt at 22 percent without a second thought, then there is a problem. When you look at your fees and finance charges, compare those each month to your gains in the market. This comparison usually makes very clear how destructive debt can be over time.

Opportunity Cost

Financial decisions are almost always about choosing one option over another. How you make those choices defines how you will live in the future. Unfortunately, many people make the mistake of allowing current or short-term financial decisions to outweigh what is good for them in the long term. This is due to a lack of understanding of opportunity cost. *Opportunity cost* is the difference in real dollars of choosing one option over another.

An example of this would be, should you pay off your debt or invest money into a retirement account? Many people have hopped on the bandwagon of becoming debt free, and I certainly agree with that thought process to a certain extent. With credit card interest rising well above the 20 percent mark, it makes sense to carry much less of that type of debt. But what if you have a student loan at 4 percent and can make a return of 8 percent or better in the stock market?

In this case, it makes sense to pay the minimum on the student loans and invest. Not only will you earn a higher rate than you are paying on the loan, but you also have to remember that student loan interest is tax deductible, which effectively brings your interest rate to zero on the loan. If you then take any additional money and invest it in a tax-advantaged investment or account, then it makes the dollars contributed more powerful due to their tax-advantaged status.

This type of example shows how important it is to not only look at the surface returns that you may get taking one option over another, but also to look at the tax consequences to determine the true value before making a decision. We are faced with opportunity cost decisions constantly, whether it be to have a latte at Starbucks versus a cup of free coffee at the office, or whether to eat out at lunch or brown-bag it. One of the major cornerstones of improving your current financial health is to understand these choices in relation to opportunity cost. Instead of seeing a dollar as just a dollar, you learn to see it for its true future value or in terms of its true cost. Let's look at an example:

Look back at the compound interest example. You can see that $1 invested at 6 percent (which is conservative) will turn into $6 over thirty years. This gives you an idea of what the dollar you are spending today is worth. If you eat out for lunch every day and it costs $9, then the real cost of that lunch is $54 taken from your retirement. If you eat out three days per week at a cost of $27 per week, then you can quickly see how the opportunity cost adds up to $162 per week. It may not seem like much now, but combined with the other financial decisions you make every day, it can add up to a substantial amount.

Now let's take it one step further and assume that you put those lunches on a credit card charging 20 percent interest and pay the minimum each month. It will take you forty-eight months to pay off the debt with added interest of at least $0.80 for each dollar. So that $9 lunch actually costs $16.20 if put on that 20 percent credit card. If you take this additional debt financing and include the opportunity cost of that amount when calculating what it means for retirement, then the cost of that lunch is amplified to $97.20. Multiply that by three times per week, and it is a total of $291.60! Would you really want to spend that amount just to eat lunch?

Of course you wouldn't, but because few people stop to calculate the true cost of some of their spending habits, they are seriously hurting themselves in the long run. I've used this example many times, and I have been told frequently that it is just a scare tactic to get people to invest. This always strikes me as an odd comment because what I'm explaining is the truth in hard numbers. If that frightens people and wakes them up to how frivolously they allow money to flow through their lives, then I'm good with that. I see it as an example of how easily you can make very subtle shifts in your spending habits and benefit not just by a few thousand dollars, but by a few hundred thousand if you really make some changes.

That is my goal: to help you understand how to help yourself to a great retirement through very small, yet significant changes in the way you understand and use money.

The Value of a Plan

The whole reason for developing a financial plan is to put it into action. You may feel like you don't have the resources to invest or that the amount you have is of such small consequence that it's hopeless. There are numerous options, and no matter your finances, there is a way to live in retirement without being destitute. Maybe you're in your fifties and haven't saved a dime. That doesn't mean all is lost. Some of the biggest hurdles to overcome are your own thoughts and beliefs, and if you convince yourself that there is no way you can ever get enough money to retire, then you won't. But if you commit to learning the options available and how they can help you reach your goals, you will find a way.

Often no matter how much you have put back for retirement, looking at the numbers compared to what you eventually will need can be a little depressing. Try to let that emotion go. You have to look at the numbers objectively and not put any undue emotion into what has, or hasn't, happened. Although it can be a little disheartening if you are not as far along as you'd hoped, consider what will happen if you don't change the situation. The only way to make your financial goals happen is though action, not avoidance.

After you have a reasonable plan to achieve your goals, you must commit to it. If you won't commit to your plan, you're just wasting your time. This means you must make it a serious priority. If something comes up, modify your plan to account for it and keep moving forward—but don't let it stop you.

You won't always think about your retirement plan, so it's important to automate the routine actions or make them habits as much as possible. In the long run, your financial habits will determine your results, so even the small decisions—like having that $9 lunch—are important.

Chapter 7

There's Advice, and Then There's Advice

One of the most interesting things about people is that they say one thing and do another. No matter how analytical you think you are, just wait until your money's involved! We use things such as the stock tip whispered over lunch or the opinion of our insurance agent or, worse yet, we listen to the media. One day the market is down, and everyone yells, "Sell!" The next day it's up, and they yell, "Buy!" This strategy is exactly backward. The object of making money through investing is to buy low and sell high. Most of us know this fact, but we still make unbelievably irrational decisions.

In 2005, a study published in *Psychological Science* reported that people with injuries to the emotional part of the brain made better trading decisions. The research team from Stanford, Carnegie Mellon University, and the University of Iowa discovered that those with normal brains often made irrational decisions based on results from the previous round. Those with injuries that blocked the emotional response made better choices.

People such as firefighters, police officers, and soldiers who are faced with what most would consider traumatic events will verify that under extreme pressure in what is normally an emotionally stressful situation, training takes over. The same is true of investing.

Investment advisers have long known that amateur investors' emotions will lead them to do the opposite of what they should be doing. They buy in a moment of market excitement, even as the experienced investors are selling. They stubbornly hold an investment, even as heavy selling points to the fact that experienced investors are abandoning ship.

If these inexperienced investors don't sell at the bottom in panic, they sell in relief when the stock gets back to their break-even point, and they often feel as if they escaped a beating. But the truth is that they should be holding the investment or buying more shares at that time—not tucking their tail and running. But try to convince an amateur investor of this! I personally know an adviser who is getting sued, not because he gave bad advice, but because he gave good advice—*five* times. He met with the client five times trying to get him not to sell in a panic. The client did it anyway, and when the market went up, he sued his adviser for not trying harder to convince him! The judge said that if the adviser was really serious, he would have fired the client. My view is that you should not be so stubborn as to force anyone to fire you. But that is the strength of our fear.

I like to watch professionals play poker on TV. The difference between a professional and an amateur poker player is the same as the difference between an experienced investor and a novice: emotion. Pros calculate the risk compared to the possible reward and make an analytical decision. They aren't attached to it, nor do they place more importance on that particular hand than it warrants. Novices, however, are a whole different story. They scare easy and hold on to losers for no logical reason. They go all in with nothing and bluff at the nuts.

Unfortunately investing isn't poker—it's the real deal. So how does an investor steer clear of his emotions and make the right decisions? The best way is to use a set of sound investing rules and follow them rather than your emotions.

These rules may include:

Create some detachment: Pretend that you will have to get up in front of a group of investors you really respect and make the argument for why you did what you did (I imagine Warren Buffet). If you don't feel comfortable with the explanation, then rethink the move. Remember facts, not feelings or gut instinct.

Rely on knowledge: If you wouldn't be able to explain your actions, you probably don't have enough knowledge to be investing, but that's okay. Everyone starts somewhere. Begin with educating yourself. Start reading, or attend seminars. Learn how to do fundamental research and how to read charts. More than anything, develop a fair amount of skepticism for what you hear and decide the facts yourself.

Choosing a Financial Adviser

Financial advisers can help you through the maze of investment choices and guide you along the path of meeting your financial goals. Unfortunately, finding a good one can be difficult. The best recommendations usually come from friends and family, but be sure that these friends and family members have had good returns and are not just recommending the advisers because they perceive them to be a nice person or attend church with them.

Advisers specialize in various areas, although most can advise you for general investing. Before you meet with any potential adviser, you should define your investment objectives, and you may have several. For example, you may want to start saving for retirement, put money away for your child's education, and set aside money for a trip to Disneyland for the family. All of these items should be discussed and prioritized.

When you do meet with a potential adviser, you should expect some basic services. These include:

- Assessment of your relevant financial history, such as tax returns, investments, retirement plans, wills, and insurance policies.

- Identification of areas where you may need assistance, such as building a retirement income or improving your investment returns.

- Determination of the appropriate level of risk based on your personality and comfort level, and a plan to manage your portfolio at that risk level.

- Discussion and preparation of a personalized financial plan based on your situation. Explanation of this plan, documented in writing, should be thorough and communicated in a simple and easy-to-understand fashion.

- Specific steps to help you implement your financial plan, including referring you to specialists, such as lawyers or accountants, if necessary.

- Minimization of tax and transactions costs.

- Periodic reviews of your situation and financial plan to monitor and suggest changes when needed.

An adviser may not be able to help you if he doesn't know what you want. It is your responsibility to make sure you provide an adviser with the information he needs to advise you appropriately. This means you shouldn't withhold information that could be important.

The first step in finding an adviser is to make a list of those who have been recommended and then perhaps add a few others whom you have heard of or who have good credentials. You will then want to make an appointment to interview these prospective advisers. The following is a list of questions that will help you gather basic information to compare the candidates. Most advisers who work for large firms or financial companies will have the basic certifications, but there are many independent financial advisers who offer fee-based advice. However, you must ascertain which companies and what products they are associated with to determine the possible motivation for the advice they give you.

- **What licenses, certificates, and registrations do you have?** These can range from insurance licenses to securities licenses and professional designations. The type and variety of licenses will determine the products the adviser can offer. For example, many insurance agents can help you set up a retirement account but can't offer individual stocks or bonds.

- **What services do you provide?** The minimum should be an evaluation of your situation and a written plan with follow-up reviews on a regular basis.

- **What kind of clients do you serve?** Some advisers specialize in working with individual clients; others specialize in the business market. If you are looking for advice in a specialized area, you want someone who has experience with your needs.

- **How many clients do you have?** Although you don't want someone who doesn't have time for you, you also don't want to be one of his only ten clients because that could indicate a problem with his business.

- **How much money do you manage?** This is referred to as *assets under management*. If the adviser has a relatively small client base but $10 million-plus in assets under management, you can surmise that he works with people with a high net worth. On the other hand, if he has one hundred clients and less than $4 million in assets under management, you can conclude that most of his clients have a much lower net worth. Depending on which category you fit into, you can decide if the adviser is for you.

- **How long have you been in the business?** Although you would like to have an experienced adviser, you must also remember that the rules and regulations of investing change constantly, and newer advisers often have the most up-to-date information. Although everyone with a financial certification is required to attend additional training every year or two, it still can leave a big gap. My advice is to look for an adviser who has been around for at least five years. Because most of them must build their own clientele if they survive beyond three years, they will most likely be around for decades.

- **How would you summarize your philosophy of money management?** You need to be clear on your idea of risk so the adviser doesn't recommend investments that you would be uncomfortable with.

- **What types of investments do you recommend?** This gives you an indication of what he can offer, although many advisers say they only offer what the clients need, so you may have to dig a little further.

- **What is your area of expertise?** You may get responses such as estates, retirement, trusts, or education planning. Many advisers handle a variety of investments, but most have one in particular that makes up the majority of their business.

- **What separates you from other advisers?** This gives you an indication of what the adviser feels his strongest attributes are.

- **What are your educational credentials and business experience?** You want to know your adviser's educational credentials and whether he has owned or currently owns a business. Contact the organizations that issued the credentials to verify whether the adviser did, in fact, earn the credentials and whether he remains in good standing with the organization. If he was an English major in college and has no business experience, you would expect him to have additional certifications to offer investment advice.

- **How does your past investment performance rank against your benchmarks and peers?** It is important to not only ask how his advice has panned out for other clients, but also to ask about what holdings your adviser has. Would you want to buy stocks from an adviser who didn't own any? I know I wouldn't.

- **What references can you give?** Not only is it important to get references from the adviser's current client base, but you must check those references.

- **What process will you use to help me with my investments?** Most companies have proprietary software that helps them provide a good plan for you, and they also have a stable of analysts who do the indepth research that is required to understand some investments.

- **How are you compensated, and how do you set your fees?** Some advisers are compensated by charging you a fee for their advice. Some are paid through commissions on the products they sell. Some use both methods. It is important to understand the financial structure for the advice they are giving you.

- **Do you have a minimum account fee or minimum investment?** This is important because different firms have different requirements.

- **If you charge a fee, what do I receive for that fee?** You should understand what is and is not included, and the adviser must offer you a disclosure of all fees and services in writing.

- **Who will review my financial affairs with me?** Some large brokerages may shift you to their newer associates if you don't have large accounts with them. If you expect personal service from the adviser giving you the advice, then you should make that expectation clear in the initial meeting.

- **Will you provide an individual financial plan?** This should always be provided in writing, no matter how little you have to invest.

- **How often do you communicate with your clients?** This will help you understand what the normal contact frequency is so your expectations are not out of line.

- **How often will the portfolio be reviewed?** This should be at least once per year for a retirement account and more frequently for shorter-term goals.

Demystifying Credentials

Many financial advisers have a variety of initials after their name that indicate their certifications. These can be confusing, so I have compiled a short list of the most common financial credentials to clarify the differences.

- **CFA—Chartered Financial Analyst:** This designation is awarded by the Association of Investment Management and Research. The CFA is a prestigious credential recognized worldwide and held mostly by institutional money managers, investment advisers, and stock analysts. Candidates must pass three (one per year) extensive and rigorous six-hour exams sequentially covering a comprehensive curriculum. They must also provide character references and agree to adhere to the Code of Ethics and Standards of Professional Conduct.

- **CFP—Certified Financial Planner:** This designation is awarded by the Certified Financial Planner Board of Standards. Candidates must pass a ten-hour exam and agree to abide by a code of ethics.

- **CLU—Chartered Life Underwriter:** This designation is given by the American College and is held mostly by life insurance agents.

- **CPA—Certified Public Accountant:** This designation is held by tax advisers and accountants who must pass a rigorous test administered nationally and receive state accountancy board approval.

- **MBA—Master of Business Administration:** This is a graduate-level degree generally seen as providing a solid financial background. Education in finance and investments will depend on the school and major field.

- **Registered Representative:** This designation is usually held by stockbrokers who must pass National Association of Securities Dealers (NASD) series exam(s). There is no explicit financial planning component to the testing.

- **RIA—Registered Investment Adviser:** This means an individual or a firm has filed with the U.S. Securities and Exchange Commission (SEC) and paid a modest fee. They are required to present a copy of the filing.

Although credentials are very important, you also should select an adviser whom you feel comfortable with, both personally and professionally. You also should be confident in the adviser's morals and ethics, which is why it is so important to understand the compensation structure so you have an idea if the adviser is promoting investments that are in your best interest or his.

Bad Managers Do Exist

Though there are many good advisers, there are also those who don't help you as much as they should. Their advice may be due to lack of experience or simply because they are not paying attention. Either way, any of the following actions by an adviser should send up a red flag:

- Choosing investments not suited to your goals and risk tolerance.

- Failing to diversify and not paying attention to the fees and costs of their recommendations.

- Reacting to short-term volatility, not long-term market movements.

- Reacting emotionally to investment decisions (big flag!).

There are other behaviors to be aware of; though they are not as obvious, they can still have devastating effects in the long term. For example, an adviser may be excessively risk averse, and by not allowing enough risk, the adviser may set up a portfolio that will result in lower returns that are not in line with your goals. By simply matching the market or not straying far from a benchmark, an adviser can reduce the risk of the investments significantly underperforming and limit his chances of getting fired. This activity protects them but doesn't get you much for your money.

In contrast, an adviser who has significantly underperformed may also exhibit behavior that is not in the client's best interest. What does a quarterback do when he's trailing at the end of a game and his back is against the wall? He throws the bomb—the Hail Mary, the long shot. Similarly, advisers who have underperformed will be tempted to take additional risk in an effort to catch up. An adviser on the verge of getting fired may take larger risks because he is likely to get fired anyway. Betting the long shot may be his last chance to keep a client.

Financial Planner or Investment Adviser?

Most financial planners are investment advisers, but not all investment advisers are financial planners. Some financial planners assess every aspect of your financial life—including savings, investments, insurance, taxes, retirement, and estate planning—and help you develop a detailed strategy or financial plan for meeting all of your financial goals. Others call themselves financial planners, but they may only be able to recommend that you invest in a narrow range of products, and sometimes those products aren't securities.

Be sure to meet potential advisers face to face to make sure you get along. And remember: many types of individuals can help you develop a personal financial plan and manage your hard-earned money. The most important thing is that you know your financial goals, have a plan in place, and check out the professional you choose using the earlier list of questions.

A Dose of Reality

It is very easy to look back on a bad turn in the financial markets and blame your financial adviser. It is not uncommon for a client to think that because a financial adviser allowed a poorly performing investment to remain in his portfolio and suffer a loss, the adviser is not working in his best interest. In most cases, nothing could be further from the truth.

For example, a retirement account has a very long time horizon, so short-term volatility should not be of any concern. In fact, it would be worse if the adviser advocated immediately dumping an investment and buying another because those would incur additional fees. Remember that transactions make money (in most cases) for the adviser, so it is hard to make the argument that he is doing you a disservice by telling you to hold onto an investment.

As long as you have a reasonably diversified portfolio that makes sense given your particular situation, it seems reasonable that your adviser would caution you against making any big changes in the short term. That's not to say that an adviser shouldn't be ready to reevaluate a strategy in light of market conditions, and perhaps even make changes. But a large part of an adviser's job is educating the client on what these market conditions really mean and preventing him from overreacting or making emotional decisions.

It is easy for anyone to play the coulda, shoulda, woulda game after the fact. If it were indeed that easy to guess the direction that investments would move, then we would all be millionaires. Advisers don't have a crystal ball and can't predict the future. They merely offer you expert advice and education, which is all anyone can really ask.

Your adviser should talk to you about your goals, as well as how much risk you're willing to take to reach them, and how you might react to market setbacks along the way. If you haven't had this sort of discussion with your adviser—and if you don't touch base periodically to reassess your situation—then I don't see how an adviser can make sensible recommendations. If your adviser tries to fit you into the same box as the rest of his clients, then you should be concerned.

For example, assume that you have a very small retirement account. You may decide you want to invest that small amount very aggressively because the rest of your investment accounts are more diversified. If your adviser gives you significant difficulty, knowing that the majority of your funds are fully diversified and that you have a long time horizon until you retire, then you have the right to ask why.

After your adviser has a good sense of your goals and risk tolerance, he can set a reasonable strategy. The foundation for that strategy should be a diversified asset mix that includes a variety of different stocks (large, small, growth, value, domestic, and foreign) or stock funds and bonds or bond funds.

The mix of assets should be designed to give you a good possibility of achieving the returns you'll need to reach your goals with a level of volatility that's acceptable to you. Although the adviser can't guarantee performance, he should be able to give you a reasonable forecast of how that portfolio might perform over the long run and, at the very least, tell you how that mix has done in good and bad markets in the past.

I like the idea of the more comprehensive financial planner who goes beyond pure investment advice and helps you look into such issues as whether you're saving enough, whether you're taking full advantage of tax breaks, and, if you're retired or nearing retirement, the odds that the money you have saved will be enough to support you throughout your retirement.

No plan is going to go exactly by the book. So your adviser or planner should provide periodic reports—most do so at least quarterly—that show you how you're doing compared to market or investment benchmarks, such as the Dow Jones Industrial Average. If your portfolio's performance is off the mark—either above or below its benchmark—then your adviser should explain why, and you should discuss whether any changes are needed.

Most good advisers will know that a big rise or fall (especially a fall) in the market will raise investor concern. To calm worries, these advisers are often proactive and will call their clients to discuss the current market and why their portfolio is or is not affected. It's not enough at times like this for an adviser to say, "Don't worry, be happy." He should be ready to go over the strategy again and make sure it's still appropriate for your situation. Most important, he should explain why the strategy still applies, even if it's losing money at the moment.

If something about your situation has changed or if it turns out you overestimated your level of risk tolerance, it could make sense to fine-tune and perhaps readjust your portfolio. Remember, though, if you're constantly making changes, you probably aren't adhering to a real strategy anyway.

If after careful consideration, you still feel that your adviser isn't measuring up, then by all means search for another one. You should never stay with an adviser who you don't have confidence in. However, if you are expecting your adviser to be perfect and predict every nuance and bobble of the market, you will never be happy or realistic in your expectations.

The balance between good advice and being pushed is that you have enough sense to let someone save you from yourself. Most investors feel compelled to fix the short-term problem and recoup losses no matter what. This is when you hear of someone losing everything—not because they made one bad mistake, but because they made one and then another and another. Don't be that person. Educate yourself and find help if needed to get you on course.

Chapter 8

I Am Investor—
Hear Me Roar!!

No matter if you are a beginner or a sophisticated investor, understanding yourself and your own risk tolerance is the key to knowing what investments may suit you. It seems that no matter what you read or hear on TV these days, everyone has a strategy or proven system for making money. In fact, they do. There are endless ways to become a millionaire through investments—but that doesn't mean that every investment is for you. Even though all investors are trying to make money, each one comes from a different background, education level, and experience, and each investor has different needs and objectives. Certain types of investments will suit you, and the way you find them is to understand two very basic things about yourself: your own investment objectives and your investing personality.

I recently spoke with Larry Sarbit, the president and CEO of Sarbit Asset Management in Winnipeg, Manitoba. Larry stated, "Everyone these days expects quick returns. They're not willing to ride out the bad times to realize long-term gains." It is essential to take your time horizon into consideration and not gamble everything on one trade.

You should consider several factors before you examine the various types of investments. These include safety of principal, current income, and capital appreciation; how you feel about these factors will depend on your age, stage in life, and personal circumstances.

For example, a seventy-two-year-old widow living off of her retirement accounts is going to be much more interested in preserving the value of her money than a thirty-two-year-old businessman would be. The woman is completely dependent on the money in those accounts and cannot risk losing that source of income. The businessman, however, has substantial cash flow from his job and knows it will be decades before he needs to live on the money he is investing for retirement. Therefore, the businessman can be much more aggressive in choosing his investments and investment strategies.

A person's overall financial health will also affect his objectives. A multimillionaire is going to have much different goals than a newly married couple just starting out. The millionaire would not think twice about investing $100,000 in the commodity market, which is considered a very risky investment. To him, this amount is a small percentage of his overall worth. Meanwhile, the young couple may be counting every penny for a down payment on a house and can't afford to risk losing their money in a risky investment. Regardless of the potential returns of a risky investment, the amount of risk is just not appropriate for the young couple.

As a general rule, the shorter your time horizon, the more conservative you should be. For instance, if you are investing primarily for retirement and you are still in your twenties, you still have plenty of time to make up for any market losses you might incur along the way. Additionally, if you start investing when you are young, you don't have to put huge chunks of your paycheck away every month because you have the power of compounding on your side.

However, if you are about to retire, it is very important that you either protect or increase the money you have accumulated. Because you will soon be accessing your investments, you don't want to expose all of your money to a great deal of market risk. You don't want the account to decrease significantly in a market slump right before you need to start accessing your assets.

A person's investment personality reflects the amount of risk that he is comfortable with. You may want to invest in a stock that everyone thinks is the best thing since sliced bread. But if you worry about it and can't sleep at night, then it's not the right investment for you. Conversely, if you look at the returns on your retirement accounts and feel frustrated, then you are probably invested too conservatively. Just like there are those who like to skydive and those who won't even step on an airplane, the types of investors run the gamut from overly conservative to extremely risky. Although you may be a little uncomfortable at first with some kinds of investments, as you gain more experience you will notice that your risk tolerance can change as well.

The most frightening circumstance for many investors is to see a huge drop in the market. You must know how much volatility you can stand before you start losing sleep. Unfortunately the only way most people find out is through trial and error. Because we have so many emotional attachments to money, the whole subject of risk can be confusing. You may consider yourself an adventurous person in every way, but when it comes to money, you have an unreasonable fear of loss. This could be due to any number of experiences or ideas you may have been taught as a child. It could also be due to financial losses you have suffered in the past.

A good example of this mind-set can be illustrated by many of the people in my grandmother's generation. Having gone through the Great Depression, they had many very conservative ideas about money and a big distrust of credit. The experiences they had and circumstances they lived through shaped this mind-set, just as the circumstances and events in your life have shaped yours.

Commitment and Aversion to Loss

We talked earlier in this book about the fact that losses affect us more emotionally than potential gain. A great illustration of this was originally printed in the book *Sway: The Irresistible Pull of Irrational Behavior* by Ori Brafman and Rom Brafman.

Independently, each of these two forces—commitment and aversion to loss—has a powerful effect on us. But when the two forces combine, it becomes much harder to break free and do something different.

This is illustrated by an exercise at Harvard Business School where Professor Max Bazerman auctions off a $20 bill. On the first day of class, Prof. Bazerman announces a game that seems innocuous enough. Waving a $20 bill in the air, he offers it up for auction. Everybody is free to bid; there are only two rules.

The first is that bids are to be made in $1 increments. The second rule is a little trickier. The winner of the auction, of course, wins the bill. But the runner-up must still honor his or her bid, while receiving nothing in return. In other words, this is a situation where second best finishes last.

Indeed, at the beginning of the auction, as people sniff out an opportunity to get a $20 bill for a bargain, the hands quickly shoot up, and the auction is officially underway. A flurry of bids follows. As Bazerman described it, "The pattern is always the same. The bidding starts out fast and furious until it reaches the $12 to $16 range."

At this point, it becomes clear to each of the participants that he or she isn't the only one with the brilliant idea of winning the twenty bucks for cheap. There is a collective hard swallow. As if sensing the floodwaters rising, the students get jittery. "Everyone except the two highest bidders drop out of the auction," Bazerman explained.

Without realizing it, the two students with the highest bids get locked in. "One bidder has bid $16, and the other has bid $17," Bazerman said. "The $16 bidder must either bid $18 or suffer a $16 loss." Up to this point, the students were looking to make a quick dollar; now neither one wants to be the sucker who paid good money for nothing. This is when the students adopt the equivalent of football's war-of-attrition model. They become committed to the strategy of playing not to lose.

Like a runaway train, the auction continues, with the bidding going up past $18, $19, and $20. As the price climbs higher, the other students don't know whether to watch or cover their eyes. "Of course," reflected Bazerman, "the rest of the group roars with laughter when the bidding goes over $20."

From a rational perspective, the obvious decision would be for the bidders to accept their losses and stop the auction before it spins out of control. But that's easier said than done. Students are pulled by both the momentum of the auction and the looming loss if they back down—a loss that is growing greater by the bid. The two forces, in turn, feed off each other: commitment to a chosen path inspires additional bids, driving the price up, making the potential loss loom even larger.

And so students continue bidding: $21, $22, $23, $50, $100, up to a record $204. Over the years that Bazerman has conducted the experiment, he has never lost a penny (he donates all proceeds to charity). Regardless of who the bidders have been—college students or business executives attending a seminar—they are always swayed. The deeper the hole they dig themselves into, the more they continue to dig.

Managing Expectations

Risk is all about expectations. Take the example of commuting to and from work. It bears a certain risk. You leave your house expecting to arrive at work on time. Anything can happen, from an accident to road construction to traffic jams, but if you travel the road frequently enough, you come to know the risks and still arrive every day at almost the same time. The point is that we become familiar and comfortable with these elements of risk because we have learned over years of commuting to accept them, and we understand when things happen that might interfere with our objective. We don't stop and turn around at the first sign of a problem.

Now think about your ideas of the financial markets. Many people see the markets as a win or a loss—an all-or-nothing proposition. In reality it is anything but. The market over time has consistently gained an average of 10 percent per year. Realize this represents an average, not an exact number. Some years you can easily earn more than 10 percent, other years you may show a loss, but overall the market increases over time. So why, then, are people so afraid? The answer is perception.

It is a well-known fact that you have a much higher chance of being killed in a car accident than in an airplane crash. Yet how many times does the risk of death cross your mind when you hop in your car? On the other hand, how many times have you encountered a little turbulence on a flight and silently hoped the airplane wouldn't fall out of the sky? Your perception of risk outweighs the reality of the risk. We are so used to the risk associated with driving because we have done it so much that we feel in control and are more than willing to accept the risk. Many people find that their ideas of financial risk are similarly out of line with the true risk that it represents.

I find it very common for people to think that investing in stocks, bonds, or any other investment vehicle is a lot riskier than it really is. Worse, most of them lack experience in financial markets, so they do not become comfortable with how they work. Everyone wants the great returns they frequently hear that the market has to offer, but they have tremendous difficulty in overcoming their fear. You must find out what return you will be comfortable earning, while still being able to accept the risk and sleep at night. Your risk tolerance is a very personal issue. Unfortunately many financial advisers, who are used to the risk, do not recognize how personal it truly is.

The key to obtaining your optimal risk-versus-reward balance is a gradual investment approach. Don't start by jumping off a cliff. Start small with perhaps a third or more of your money in conservative investments and then reevaluate every three to six months, gradually reallocating that money into investments that earn a higher return. I usually recommend that a beginning or inexperienced investor try this progressive investing strategy and then take the investing process at his own pace. Gather experience before moving on to riskier investments and understand what you feel comfortable with. Larry Sarbit also said, "Lack of patience and too much emotion are two of the biggest problems today in investing." Go with what you are comfortable with and don't let your emotions lead.

Taking care of your money and investing for financial security should never be a burden. If you are worried and constantly consumed with fear, then it's time to step back and be a bit more conservative for a while longer. Don't be afraid to take a step back if you feel overwhelmed. This is your money, and no one can tell you what is right for you.

When the Market Goes South

Part of understanding yourself is understanding how you will react when the market declines. If you switch on CNN and see that the market has dropped by a few hundred points, how will you feel? Will you be calm, knowing that this is a normal part of the cycle, or will you immediately panic and pull your money out? The fearful investor will pull his money out, while the cautious investor will adopt a wait-and-see attitude. An experienced investor, however, will continue to add to his investment account because he knows that anything he buys during the downturn will actually gain more when the market goes back up. According to Larry Sarbit, "The media contributes to the short-term problem. If you tune into CNBC, they're always talking about something that's happening right now, this very minute. How does that contribute to long-term investing?"

Declines of more than 10 percent in the major stock market indexes do happen on occasion and are part of the economic cycle. Even when there is talk of recession or hard times ahead, you must remember that you are in for the long haul, so a downturn in one or two years is to be expected. While it's easy for me to say that, I also know what it's like to pull up your investment account and see the numbers declining. The only thing that keeps you from overreacting is having confidence in the market and becoming familiar with its occasional volatility.

Several behaviors can indicate that you are overly concerned about a market that is in a slump, and the first is to be obsessively focused on it. Are you turning on the financial news every few minutes to hear the latest from the floor of the exchange, or are you spending numerous hours clicking through every article on the Internet concerning the downturn? Constantly obsessing is really just a sign of fear, and taking in more and more bad news each day does nothing but enhance your emotional turmoil. Wean yourself off of the constant analysis and relax. Your money is in for the long haul, so what difference does it make if a particular company downgrades its fourth-quarter projections?

It is important to understand that the financial media, like any other media, look for the stories that are going to offer the most interest for viewers. Unfortunately that usually involves some sort of scandal, financial bad news, or economic recession. All of these play on your emotional fears because you perceive that every bit of news they broadcast affects your money—and it doesn't. They are reporting the most interesting news, not necessarily the most important news for your particular situation, so don't allow yourself to get overwhelmed by everything you hear.

You should also know that just because some analyst or guru on TV (or radio) downgrades a stock, that doesn't mean it's forever ruined. He is just giving his opinion of the current financial situation of the company, and that situation changes all the time, as does the guru's opinion, which depends on market conditions. The expert may have other reasons for his particular opinion depending on the company he works for or how he is compensated. So it is always good to listen, but be slightly skeptical of anyone who thinks he has the right answers. If the experts were always right, they'd be millionaires themselves, and very few analysts or brokers are.

It is interesting that at the same time that many people are overreacting to the market volatility and downturns, they're underreacting to other areas of their financial lives. They accumulate more debt than they can manage and spend their money in even more frivolous ways. It is a strange and intriguing facet of the human brain that when we worry about money, we also tend to do things that keep us from having it. Some people shop, some gamble, some simply refuse to pay attention to where their money goes. Fear can be very motivating, but it can also lead to paralysis that prevents us from really understanding what we are doing and why. You must know when to take action to improve your financial health and when to stay the course. The problem is that the right answer can *feel* wrong.

In most investing, the timeline is long. For this reason, when the market goes down, the best thing to do is to stay put or add more money. No matter how savvy you think you are, when faced with this situation, you may know the right answer, but putting in money or leaving it alone when you see the numbers declining can feel very wrong. If your investments are diversified and you don't plan to touch the money for a couple of decades at least, it doesn't make sense to overreact to a few months of volatility and sell everything. Although it's stressful at times watching your money shrink, you must also be aware that putting all of your money into very low-risk investments will create an opposite but equally devastating problem: your money won't earn enough to meet your goals.

Some investors think that they will pull out of their investments now and then hop back in when the market goes up. This is called *timing the market*, and if it were that easy to do, then every investment would be a sure thing. The truth is that you are much more likely to lose more money by hopping in and out of the market than by consistently saving over time. The same fear that prods you to get out of volatile investments also prevents you from getting back in again until they are already on a high. So the only logical direction they will go is down, and then you feel like you have to get out again. This is a vicious cycle that you should never allow yourself to fall into because it will seriously damage your chance at long-term success.

Forest for the Trees

It is very easy to become wrapped up in investment performance, especially if the market is making big moves either up or down, but that does not give you an excuse to stop paying attention to the rest of your finances. Millions of people are struggling with an overload of debt or with an adjustable-rate mortgage that has reset to a much higher level. When faced with bad news about debt, the typical reaction is to freeze and want to do nothing, somehow hoping the problem will ease up by itself or go away.

The first sign of this type of behavior is putting off one bill to pay another. My grandmother would call this robbing Peter to pay Paul, and as debt load increases, this solution seems the only way to keep everything afloat. Unfortunately it is usually the beginning of a downward spiral because your debts continue to increase and your ability to pay them decreases. By the time you realize the enormity of the problem, it becomes overwhelming.

I generally advocate that everyone be as proactive as possible in these situations. If your credit card rate jumps, call the card issuer immediately—not a month or two down the road. If the company doesn't lower the rate, look for another card. Don't wait until the balance gets so big that it affects your credit score. The same is true of an adjustable-rate mortgage. You know well in advance if it is due to be reset. The time to negotiate with the lender is *before* the rate resets so it is aware that you are willing to work with it. Trying to negotiate when you are thirty or sixty days late with a payment puts you in a much weaker position.

The time to correct any negative financial situation is immediately and efficiently, instead of waiting until your choices are limited. Feeling financially helpless and hopeless has forced many people to liquidate what little retirement savings they have to catch up—and the penalties and taxes destroy everything they have worked to build.

Another way you can become blind to what is going on in the rest of your financial life is to become overconfident in your investments. If you happen to hit an upswing and have investments rise very quickly, you may feel an excitement that leads you to believe that you are more experienced than you are. It often helps to talk to a very experienced investor on occasion who may remember the tech stock bubble of the early 1990s or the real estate downturn in the 1980s. This will give you a better perspective. We have all read or heard the disclaimer from financial companies that says, "Past performance is not a guarantee of future gain." This should warn you that no matter how good things look, you should be aware that it is usually temporary, and you are better to assume modest gains over many years than to try to hit the jackpot.

The tech bubble from the early '90s is a great example of stocks in one sector climbing so high that people put every dime they had into them, only to see the sector come crashing down. You would think that they should have known better, but it is hard not to believe the best when things are going well. As humans, we put the most belief in recent experience instead of relying on historical fact. This can get us into much trouble in the investment world. An investor can fall into the trap of feeling invincible, and when the fall comes, it can hurt.

Asset Allocation and Risk Diversification

Everyone has heard that they shouldn't put all of their eggs in one basket. This is especially true when investing. Putting all or most of your money into one type of investment is extremely risky because you are betting that nothing negative will ever happen, and if it does, you will bear the full weight of that negative event.

Even if you are not an experienced investor, you have probably heard about asset allocation and diversification, though you may not know the difference between the two. *Asset allocation* refers to the percentage of your money you put into each type of asset category, such as stocks, bonds, and real estate. *Diversification* refers to the relative risk levels of the various investments and how they are correlated to one another.

Asset Allocation

Determining the mix of assets that are right for you and suit your goals can be challenging and is different for every person. No matter what you determine that mix to be today, you must also be aware that the mix can and should change as you age and as your goals change. The two main areas to look at in determining the best asset mix for you include your personal risk tolerance and how long your investments have to grow before you need them.

Risk tolerance is how much you can lose without panicking. No matter what investment you choose, it will have some risk. Your level of acceptance of possible loss in return for potential gain will allow you to categorize the type of investor you are. A person with a high risk tolerance is considered aggressive and does not lose sleep if he loses some ground in the process. A conservative investor generally leans toward investments that will preserve his capital and expose the money to the least amount of risk possible.

Time is an important factor in considering how to allocate your investments. If you need the money in six months, you will invest it very differently than if you plan to use the money twenty-five years from now when you retire. Because time works to your benefit, you know that you can take more risk with money that won't be used for decades. Any losses can be recouped over that time, and the potential gain can be tremendous.

Risk and Reward—Strange Bedfellows

Risk and reward are like two sides to the same coin. There can never be one without the other, and they follow each other step for step. This means that a low-risk investment will undoubtedly produce low returns. A high-risk investment also has the potential to produce high returns.

Although no investment is completely without risk, you must understand the level of risk before you put your money into any investment. Stocks, bonds, and CDs are the most common asset categories, but you can also invest in businesses and real estate, as well as many other types of investments. Investments in these asset categories typically have category-specific risks.

By investing in more than one asset category, for example stocks and bonds, you reduce the risk that you'll lose money, and your portfolio's overall investment returns will not be as volatile. If one asset category's return falls, you'll be in a position to offset those losses with better returns in another asset category.

Asset allocation is a key factor in determining whether you will reach your financial goals. If you don't include enough risk in your portfolio, your investments may not earn a large enough return to meet your financial goals. For example, if you are saving for a long-term goal, such as retirement, most financial experts would suggest that you include at least some stock or stock mutual funds in your portfolio. On the other hand, if you include too much risk in your portfolio, the money for your goal may not be there when you need it because of the potential losses you may suffer. A portfolio heavily weighted in stock or stock mutual funds, for instance, would be inappropriate for a short-term goal, such as saving for a trip you want to take within the next year.

Determining the most advantageous asset allocation for financial goals is a complicated task because it is a constantly moving target. Circumstances and conditions are always changing, so you may need to reassess your choices every few months. The trick is to pick a mix of assets that has the highest probability of meeting your goal at a level of risk you can live with. As you get closer to meeting your goal, you'll need to adjust the asset mix to preserve the gains you have enjoyed and not risk large losses.

If you are comfortable with the idea of asset allocation, you may feel confident choosing the investments that suit you. You can also get some ideas by searching the Internet for asset allocation models. Many large financial firms have websites with retirement calculators and asset allocation suggestions, given your age and goal. A financial adviser can also help to allocate your money between investments.

Although asset allocation involves spreading money among various asset classes of investment, diversification pays attention to the risk each individual investment presents and spreads that risk to investments that counterbalance one another. This means that if one investment loses money, others will make money, so the overall losses are minimized.

A diversified portfolio should be diversified both in asset categories and within asset categories. If your portfolio is allocated among stocks, CDs, and real estate, you should be invested in several stocks (for example at least twelve to fifteen), not just one. You should be invested in CDs of various interest rates and maturities, and you should own several properties that produce different returns.

As you can imagine, this can get complicated, and many investors find it easy to simply own mutual funds that are already diversified among many company stocks. Some investors may find it easier to diversify within each asset category through the ownership of mutual funds rather than through individual investments from each asset category. However, you must also know that if your mutual fund invests in only one sector of stocks, like tech stocks, you are not really diversified and may need to invest in several mutual funds to be sure you don't place yourself at unnecessary risk.

Within asset categories, that may mean considering large-company stock funds, for instance, as well as some small-company and international stock funds. Among asset categories, that may mean considering stock funds, bond funds, and money market funds. Of course, as you add more investments to your portfolio, you'll likely pay additional fees and expenses, which will, in turn, lower your investment returns. So you need to consider these costs when deciding the best way to diversify your portfolio.

Making It Easy

For those who want to make the most of their investments but don't really have the time to research every detail of a particular stock, investment companies have created mutual funds designed to take care of diversification for you. These products are known as *lifecycle funds*. A lifecycle fund is a diversified mutual fund that automatically shifts toward a more conservative mix of investments as it approaches a particular year in the future, known as its *target date*. A lifecycle fund investor picks a fund with the right target date based on her particular investment goal. The fund managers then make all decisions about asset allocation, diversification, and rebalancing. It's easy to identify a lifecycle fund because its name will likely refer to its target date. For example, you might see lifecycle funds with names like "Portfolio 2015," "Retirement Fund 2030," or "Target 2045." These funds can offer a solution for the investor who wants to diversify yet has limited time and energy to put into choosing the investments.

Age Considerations and Rebalancing Your Portfolio

It is important to reevaluate your asset allocations as you get closer to your financial goal. For those investing for retirement, you will want to preserve your gains and not be overly aggressive because you will need that money to live on in the near future. Most people investing for retirement lower the percentage of stock and add more bonds and cash equivalents as they get closer because stocks produce a higher risk. You may also reassess your allocation if your financial situation changes or if you must access the money sooner because of illness or disability.

Over time, it is normal for some investments to grow faster than others. This can result in your portfolio getting out of balance and out of alignment with your financial goals. By rebalancing to your original asset mix, you ensure that your portfolio does not overemphasize one or more asset categories, and you return your portfolio to a comfortable level of risk.

For example, say you determined that your stock investments should represent 30 percent of your portfolio. However, over the last two years, the investment properties in your portfolio have had significant gains in value as well as rental cash flow, and they now represent 60 percent. You will need to either sell one of the properties and reallocate that money to other assets or move money into other assets to counterbalance the gains in the property.

When you rebalance, you also need to review the investments within each asset allocation category. If any of these investments are out of alignment with your investment goals, you need to make changes to bring them back to their original allocation within the asset category.

You can rebalance your portfolio in one of three ways:

1. You can sell off investments from overweighted asset categories and use the proceeds to purchase investments for underweighted asset categories.

2. You can purchase new investments for underweighted asset categories.

3. If you are making continuous contributions to the portfolio, you can alter your contributions so more money goes to underweighted asset categories until your portfolio is back in balance.

Before you rebalance your portfolio, you should consider whether the method of rebalancing you choose will trigger transaction fees or tax consequences. Your financial professional or tax adviser can help you identify ways that you can minimize these potential costs.

You should reevaluate your portfolio on a six- or twelve-month interval, and because most account custodians send out statements on a quarterly basis, this is easy to remember.

Chapter 9

Two Steps Forward ...

Bankruptcy? Medical issues? Divorce (or two or three)? There are many and wide-ranging reasons for financial disasters, which can feel like the end of the world. People lose their jobs, suffer the death of a spouse, or encounter a natural disaster, such as a fire, flood, or hurricane, that can completely disrupt the plans they had for their lives. The trauma that individuals suffer due to circumstances can be all-consuming, and getting through the next day can become the biggest challenge you can face. Eventually, though, you will move on and start to put your life back together, and this includes your finances.

Even if it feels like your finances are barely on life support, you can recover from financial devastation and still plan to have some kind of investment portfolio. The biggest problem I run into with individuals who have struggled with money for whatever reason is their tendency to give up. Because we attach so much emotion to money, those emotions can convince us that there is no hope—so why try?

Now make no mistake that there are also self-inflicted financial disasters. Have you ever known anyone who cashed out their retirement savings to start their dream business only to have it fail? It happens. No one has a crystal ball to see how a particular financial decision will come out, and we all make mistakes. If you have been through something like this, it can be even harder because there is a tremendous amount of guilt associated with failing financially.

When recovering from a disaster of circumstance or poor financial decision, you need to understand that recovery is not an overnight process and does take time—but it can be done. Awareness of the problem is the first step. Don't stick your head in the sand and hope for the best because it just won't happen if you don't change things.

Whether the disaster is a hurricane, fire, or flood; a devastating accident or illness; a difficult divorce; or sudden unemployment, it's important to know how to get back to basics financially. Even if you are doing well right now, life can be unpredictable, and a little preparation now can go a long way, should you suddenly find yourself plunged into a full-scale crisis with severe financial consequences.

Also understand the suggestions I am making are just that. You can travel many paths to get back on firm financial ground and start investing again to meet your goals.

The Basics

When you're faced with a money crisis, you first have to evaluate your resources—not what you might have, but what actually exists in hard numbers. Do you have an emergency fund? If so, how long do you have before it will run out? How many items in your budget can you do without until you have more income coming in?

Now you can look at other sources of help. If you were laid off, you may be eligible for unemployment benefits; if you were injured on the job, workers' compensation may help bridge any financial gap. Do you have disability insurance through work? Is there a severance package from your former employer? Can other family members contribute income from a job or savings? Borrow only as a last resort, and before you dip into investments, take a careful look at the income tax and penalties associated with each one before you act. The cost could be greater than you think.

Now may be the time to have an open and honest discussion with your family and include them in the process of setting spending priorities. Their cooperation in trimming spending while you regroup is essential to getting through a rough financial time. Adjusting to the fact that you can't spend the way you used to is one of the greatest challenges in managing any financial crisis, but you can't continue to live that former lifestyle until you have the income to go with it. Trying to keep up appearances will lead to more devastation. Create a plan for paying your essential bills, and then cut back, eliminate, or postpone other expenditures.

As soon as you know that you will have limited resources, the best course of action concerning your creditors is to let them know. Many will allow you to set up a temporary payment plan, but you must contact them before you miss payments or make late payments. Determine an amount you can pay consistently until your finances improve, and then pay that regularly. Be realistic. If you fail to follow though on your agreement, your creditors may seek other avenues for repayment—and they can be aggressive.

Take advantage of any job training, counseling, money-management courses, state programs, or community resources that can assist you in resolving your financial difficulties. If your debts become unmanageable, then it's time to get help. This may be in the form of a mastermind group, mentor, or financial coaching program. Coping with the stresses and demands of a job loss, natural disaster, or financial crisis is never easy, and recovery can seem almost impossible. However, numerous resources are available to get you back on your feet. It's important to avoid making quick decisions that you may regret later.

For most people, it's not one big financial disaster—it's a culmination of small decisions. The easy monthly payments that convince us that we can accumulate more stuff. The car payment, the boat payment, the country club, the Ginsu knives you can buy at 3:00 am for three easy payment of $29.95. It's easy and common to become overcommitted, and instead of the instant panic of a financial disaster, it layers payment upon payment until you're stretched to the max and walk around barely able to breathe, as if there is an elephant on your chest.

The problem is that many of the payments and expenses you take on without much thought are fixed and nonvariable. They eat away at your bottom line each month, and you have fewer resources to draw upon. It only takes one very small event at that point, even something as minor as a traffic fine, to destroy your financial house of cards.

Financial overcommitment has plagued almost everyone at some point. It's much like overeating—we all do it on occasion, but that doesn't mean you have to continue down that path. Numerous items can bite you if you are not careful, and they include:

1. **A more expensive house than you can afford.** This one is very common, especially in areas where the home prices are relatively high. There is a reason that many mortgage companies have a guideline that no more than 30 percent of your income should be spent on your home. Even with the other basic expenses of living, it can be very difficult to pay other bills if your mortgage—which doesn't go away—takes up more than this percentage of your income. A home is an ongoing commitment, and maxing out what you can afford is a recipe for disaster.

2. **Car payments that stretch you to the limit.** Everyone would like to drive the latest and greatest vehicle, and it can be easy to let the salesperson convince you that the payments aren't that big—but they aren't the ones making the payment. These days, the actual payment for the car isn't the only concern. Fuel efficiency is also a key factor. If you plan your life to the penny, a 20-cent rise in gas prices can destroy your budget.

3. **Keeping up with the neighbors.** It's really a cliché, but keeping up with the Joneses is a bad omen for your finances. This can include buying the right boat, having the right vacation home, sending the kids to the right private school, or belonging to the most exclusive clubs. All of these are lifestyle choices and can steal money from what could have been a very comfortable investment portfolio. Evaluate why you are making particular choices, and if you realize it is for appearances, then understand that appearances won't pay your bills when you are seventy-five.

4. **The little things.** Numerous small expenses that you accumulate and pay on an ongoing basis add up to more than you realize. Extended cable or satellite services when you spend little time in front of the TV can be unnecessary, as are some convenience expenses, like house cleaning, lawn mowing, or memberships. The point here is not to live like a pauper, but to evaluate what you use and need, instead of habitually paying for things that serve no purpose.

The issue of overcommitment is compounded if you have large swings in income or if you receive large payments, as in seasonal work. Many commissioned salespeople become overcommitted because they occasionally receive very large checks and feel very wealthy—for a short time. When the cash is flowing freely, it is very easy to commit to more payments and a better lifestyle than you can actually afford.

Learning to live on a set amount of money each month, no matter how high your actual income that month, is a very important skill that can be learned, but sometimes it is a painful lesson. This is why self-employment can be financially difficult for some people. You must be very committed to a financial plan and very disciplined in its execution. We all have a tendency to spend exactly what we make, and this hits very hard for the self-employed person because that income is frequently uncertain and can swing dramatically.

After you recognize that you are overcommitted, there are only two effective plans of attack. One is to earn more money, and while this may temporarily relieve the problem, it will work only if you don't commit to spending even more when more cash is coming in. For many people who are overcommitted, making more money in the short term is not possible. The only option they have is to say no: no to the car, no to the house cleaning, no to the big house. Although some of these commitments may be easier to undo than others, if you stay overcommitted, you will lose it all anyway. You must make the tough decisions.

I had a client who got divorced and had business obligations that included $30,000 in radio advertising. She was proactive and contacted her creditors, setting up a plan to pay them in full over time. She met that goal, and they are all still happily doing business with her. Realize that most everyone has had financial problems of their own at some point, so they know what it's like and appreciate you being honest and proactive.

You can take several steps if you find yourself facing a disaster or are just overcommitted and drowning in debt. Set aside the blame and causes, and deal with the issue head on.

More Money Than Month

Get Organized!

Getting organized is very important when you are trying to recover financially. If the disaster is losing a job, then part of your new to-do list needs to be looking for a job immediately, rather than taking a few days to feel bad about it. One of the big dangers of losing a job, especially if it had seemed a secure job, is sinking into a depression that makes it harder to fight back and get a new position. You have to know what you have on hand, so gather up all of your statements and bills and see exactly what you have to work with.

Discipline

Yes, I said the 'D' word. You must be disciplined to survive financially—even if discipline has been a foreign concept to you in the past. If you are in debt, you have finite resources to take care of that debt, so you must either unload some of it or make more money. Staying the same only increases the problem.

Step Away from Denial

You cannot keep rolling merrily along as if nothing is happening. Avoiding the issues doesn't make them go away. Denial may include things like not opening bills, not opening bank statements, and not checking balances at the ATM. It can also mean not sharing the problem with significant others in your life. Some people hide expenses from their partner or spouse, which makes the problem even harder to deal with.

Don't Panic

Don't put your family on bread and water; be reasonable. Try to look at the situation objectively and identify the real problems. Cutting back on things like food and gas may seem like the easy solution, but the real problem may be that you're putting those expenses on credit cards and running up debt you can't pay. You must also continue to pay your bills. Skipping or rotating payments will seriously hurt your credit score and increase your overall debt obligations down the road.

This Too Shall Pass

One of the biggest psychological obstacles to financial survival is thinking that you will not survive. It's that old adage: if you think you can, then you can, but if you think you can't, then you can't. Debt can bring tremendous stress and strain to any relationship. Money problems are often cited as a cause of relationship breakdown. You must realize that money problems are temporary and completely within your control. You can and will survive them, and you want to be sure your relationships survive them as well.

Be Prepared

As they say, the best defense is a good offense. Prepare yourself now for financial challenges you may face in the future. Put back an emergency fund and use it for *emergencies*, not the vacation to Disneyland. Keep your revolving debt at a low level—not a manageable level. Manageable is a moving target and tends to rise without our noticing. Low is less than 30 percent. This will give you room to maneuver if the worst should happen.

Take Little Steps

Feeling overwhelmed is normal, but it's not an excuse. Paying back a mountain of debt may seem impossible, yet when broken down into a series of stages, it becomes possible. Think about when you bought your house. Remember the page you signed that showed the total amount of debt over the life of the loan, which was roughly three times the actual amount of the house? Wow, what an eye-opener. But if you make your payments, you will eventually own the house. The same is true of other debt in your life. If you make changes, such as not running up more debt, and start to chip away at the mountain, it will move. Taking small steps is vital in overcoming big problems.

Sometimes it's hard to know exactly how we get ourselves in so deep without noticing. It is much like the fact that if you put a frog into a pot of water and heat it slowly, the frog will boil to death without even realizing it—and that's certainly how it feels sometimes when your finances are out of control.

Planning for investing requires much more than putting some money in savings. You must pay close attention to your finances and make room for investing. It's not about just putting away the extra that you can scrape together. It's about making your future a priority, rather than blindly tripping through life hoping for the best.

No matter your age, you can employ several strategies that will help make your life more enjoyable and much less stressful. As you begin to take control, you will have an elevated sense of empowerment and control over your future. This translates into more empowerment in your everyday finances.

Chapter 10

It's Your Money!

Although we would like to think of ourselves as discerning, intelligent beings, the truth is that we get many of our beliefs about investing from what we read or from those around us. Although this isn't necessarily bad, we may adopt certain ideas or make decisions that don't really help us get ahead. These ideas can even be perpetuated and passed down to our children and grandchildren, so they will have the same beliefs and habits about money that we do. When you think of how you relate to money and realize that your views can affect future generations, you need to be sure that your views are objective and allow for the best return on investment in a given situation.

A few areas of investing tend to be surrounded by confusion and tall tales. You may recognize some of these in your own life or in the lives of those around you. Some of these ideas are even perpetuated in the media, which highlights the fact that you must be very discerning about what you hear on TV or radio, and be careful about believing everything you read—especially on the Internet.

How many times have you seen a mutual fund or other investment tout a particular return and then looked at your own investment statement, and somehow, that same investment didn't perform as well for you? What's the deal? Why can't you make the math work? The returns you see often don't take into account several factors that are directly related to you and your investments. The company or financial firm can advertise a particular return that does not take into account certain fees and other costs you must pay. You will usually find a legal explanation of this in the fine print of the advertised return. What it really means is that what you see isn't necessarily what you get, so you must determine your real return on an investment to be able to compare it to other opportunities.

There are several steps to calculating your real return, and the number that most people seek is the *annualized rate of return*. This is the overall return gained over the course of the year that takes into consideration how much you started with, what amounts were contributed over the year and when, as well as the cumulative compounding effect of those various amounts.

To calculate the return for your investment, you need to have answers to some basic questions:

1. What are the upfront costs (if any) associated with the investment, such as commissions, closing costs (for real estate), or an account setup fee if this is a new account?

2. What are the ongoing maintenance and service fees?

3. Are there research or consulting fees?

4. How time-consuming is this investment?

Costs can include things such as commissions, fees paid to financial advisers for their time, and one-time and recurring account fees. For investments such as real estate, costs may include inspections, closing costs, and loan fees. List all the fees you can find on past account statements for the year and any other fees you can think of that aren't listed. Don't forget to include how much of your time it takes to manage the investment. Some investments, like real estate, take much more personal involvement than others, such as mutual funds, and your time is valuable.

The whole idea of making money with any investment is buying low and selling high. So if some gain is good, then more is better—right? With this logic, many people convince themselves that they can time the market, meaning they can identify when the market is about to make a big swing and take advantage of it. Now really? If this were an effective investing strategy, then we would all have the money to show for it. So why do people try to do it? It's the lure of making big bucks with little effort, the great deal, the big score. Everyone wants to be better than average, but the truth is that this strategy is a big risk with very little chance of paying off consistently. Sure you might hit one great deal, but you also might hit a whole lot of really crappy ones. Proponents of this technique always want to tell you about their great deal, but a little questioning on how many of their deals have fallen flat will shut them up pretty quickly.

I've also met the market-timing gurus who are all about selling you their "system" so you too can hit it big. Most of their cash flow comes from sales—not investing—so the buyer should beware about any "system" that can time the market.

Many investment advisers are proponents of *dollar cost averaging*. This is the idea that you buy stocks or mutual funds at regular intervals, usually monthly, which allows you to average your cost and do better long term in the market. But is this true? Again, this is one of those yes-and-no answers.

Dollar cost averaging theoretically reduces market risk through the systematic purchase of stocks or mutual funds at predetermined intervals and in set amounts. Many successful investors practice this without realizing it, and other investors choose this method because it is automatic and doesn't require much thought or decision making on their part. Rather than put a lump sum into a given investment, they purchase shares over time and spread the cost basis over several years. This may provide some protection against variations in market prices. Those who use this method are most excited when the market goes down. Because they have averaged down their cost basis, there doesn't need to be much of a rise for them to recover and move into positive territory. However, when the market is skyrocketing, they often see less of a gain than they would like because they bought in incremental amounts over time, including while prices were rising.

Having said that, dollar cost averaging is great for the investor who does not already have a lump sum and is trying to accumulate wealth. Small amounts really do add up, and for many people, this systematic investing is the most effective way to add to their savings and make it a habit. Of course, this is probably not anything new for a knowledgeable investor.

The hardest part of planning for long-term financial security is trying to guess what resources will or will not exist by the time you get there. The safest course of action is to take care of yourself and use as many sources as possible to create a solution that is workable with you and not dependent on any governmental system that is destined to change.

More Money Than Month

The biggest difference between the 1950s and now is that back then, people didn't worry about retiring. They thought they'd be taken care of. Now we know differently. Yet I frequently see people who would prefer to put their heads in the sand and pretend that things will be fine. They don't really have a plan, haven't determined how they want to live, and have no idea how much money they will need. This is more common than you might think. If someone has the feeling that there's nothing she can do about it anyway, it's easy to avoid discussions of saving or financial planning. It's also easy to get caught up in everyday life and let time slide by. There are no guarantees, and there are no quick fixes. The bottom line is that no one will ever care about your financial security if you don't.

You may be shocked at the number of people who do no planning but buy a lottery ticket each week. It is not so much the action itself but the mind-set behind the action that is the most telling. These individuals put off saving or investing because they feel pressured from all sides—their mortgage is rising, gas is going up, the kids are growing and needing things. There never seems to be enough to go around, and money runs out before the end of the month. But is that reality? Each and every action you take during the course of a day may seem insignificant, but they do add up. Let's take the example of playing the lottery.

About half of American adults spend $45 billion annually on some 35,000 lottery games in forty states, plus the District of Columbia, Puerto Rico, and the U.S. Virgin Islands. But given the odds, which for the Mega Millions recently were 1 in 135,145,920, what makes anyone think he can win? Yet people still play. In fact, the average player spends $150 a year on lottery tickets, according to a recent National Survey on Gambling. Some states have averages several times higher than that.

In a 1999 survey by the Consumer Federation of America and financial services firm Primerica, 40 percent of Americans with incomes between $25,000 and $35,000 (and nearly half of respondents with an income of $15,000 to $25,000) thought winning the lottery would give them their retirement nest egg. Overall, 27 percent of respondents said their best chance to gain $500,000 in their lifetime was through a sweepstakes or lottery win, the survey said.

But think about that. If you take that $150 per year and put it into an investment account at age thirty and get an average of 8 percent return over thirty-five years, you'll have $28,000 by age sixty-five. So what? How much good does $28,000 do? Remember that it is based on $150 *per year*, which is $12.50 per month or $2.90 per week. If you invested $28.86 every week, that figure would climb to $280,000. At $57.70 per week, it would be $560,000. There's half a million dollars—and it's a sure thing, not a 1-in-135-million shot. The numbers are even better if you start young. If you start at the age of twenty-one and invest as little as $23 per week, you would also have $500,000 when you reached age sixty-five.

Hey! You're already spending everything that you earn. How are you supposed to find another $58 per week to spare? That's where deciding what you really want becomes important. Life is all about choices, and every day we make many choices without even realizing how they affect our lives. I know you've probably been told that to invest and do well, you have to sacrifice, and for some people the idea of saving $251 each month can seem like a large amount—but let's do a little math:

$58 per week ($251 per month) = $8.28 per day

Hmmm, $8.28. How many ways can you save that amount in a day? How is that going to affect your week? Here's one scenario:

Monday: Bring your lunch.

Tuesday: Skip the latte and muffin.

Wednesday: Carpool and save two gallons of gas.

Thursday: Rent a DVD instead of going to the movies.

Friday: Have one fewer drink at happy hour.

Saturday: Take a walk around the park instead of going to the gym.

Sunday: Cook at home instead of eating out.

More Money Than Month

Does that list really look like a sacrifice? No. In fact it would hardly even be noticed. Yet saving just that small amount—less than $10 per day—could give you $500,000 by the time you're sixty-five, and a great deal of peace of mind in the meantime. What seems like a small amount today can literally change your life.

The next time you're tempted to buy a lottery ticket instead of saving that dollar for your own financial security, remember that you are choosing to trade a one-in-a-million chance for a sure thing.

These are just a few of the ideas that can get in the way of your financial security. Many more are out there, any one of which could cost you big in the long run. In a perfect world, we would be surrounded by those offering to help and guide us with altruistic motives and our best benefit in mind. Unfortunately, this is not the world we live in. This does not mean that you should not seek financial advice; you should. But you should also be aware of the motivation of the person giving that advice and weigh that against what is in your best interest.

After you realize how many options you really have in retirement, the world opens up to your imagination. Knowing you can go, do, or be anything you want at this stage of the game is fun and exciting.

In the end, you are responsible for your own future—and that's a good thing. You have control, and you make the decisions. Though the learning curve may be steep at times, understanding the basics of how investing works will give you the confidence to travel your own path and ultimately have a great life, which is the most important goal.

So what happened to Charles? Charles persevered through the tough times and stuck to his plan. At one time, he had two credit cards—one that worked and one that didn't, and he never knew which was which. As he grew his multiple streams of income (MSIs), he suffered the embarrassment of not having cash flow and having his credit denied. Still, he didn't dip into that nest egg.

Todd Dean

Over time, Charles became a top salesman for a company that works almost exclusively with a top retailer in the nation, and he earns a high six-figure income. He rose through the multilevel marketing ranks to have a consistent five-figure monthly income as well. His assets have grown into the millions. Charles became that rock that everyone in his family could depend on, and most of them have accepted his help at one time or another. I asked Charles what the most important aspect of wealth accumulation was, and this was his response:

"If I've learned anything, it's that it's not about the money. It's about relationships and the people you love and being able to enjoy them. Money helps with that, but making a lot of it is not as hard as people think it is, and it's not as easy as I make it sound. It takes some doing, but if I can do it—a former alcoholic misfit with nothing to offer—then anyone can."

Visit Dean Global Group at

www.tdean.com

Sign up for our free newsletter and free webinars that include more tips and techniques for ensuring your long term financial survival in tough economic times.

See Todd Dean LIVE!
A list of upcoming cities and dates may be found at…

www.tdean.com

Dean Global Group offers individual financial management coaching and wealth creation programs. Corporate programs are also available. For more information please contact:

todd@tdean.com

Other Books from LifeSuccess Publishing

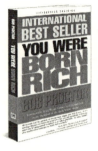

You Were Born Rich

Bob Proctor
ISBN # 978-0-9656264-1-5

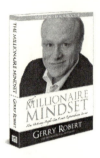

The Millionaire Mindset
How Ordinary People Can Create Extraordinary Income

Gerry Robert
ISBN # 978-1-59930-030-6

Rekindle The Magic In Your Relationship
Making Love Work

Anita Jackson
ISBN # 978-1-59930-041-2

Finding The Bloom of The Cactus Generation
Improving the quality of life for Seniors

Maggie Walters
ISBN # 978-1-59930-011-5

The Beverly Hills Shape
The Truth About Plastic Surgery

Dr. Stuart Linder
ISBN # 978-1-59930-049-8

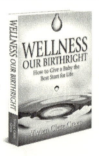

Wellness Our Birthright
How to give a baby the best start in life.

Vivien Clere Green
ISBN # 978-1-59930-020-7

Lighten Your Load

Peter Field
ISBN # 978-1-59930-000-9

Change & How To Survive In The New Economy
7 steps to finding freedom & escaping the rat race

Barrie Day
ISBN # 978-1-59930-015-3

Other Books from LifeSuccess Publishing

The Secret To Cracking
The Property Code
*7 Timeless Principles for
Successful Real Estate
Investment*

Richard S.G. Poole
ISBN # 978-1-59930-063-4

Why My Mother Didn't
Want Me To Be Psychic
*The Intelligent Guide To The
Sixth Sense*

Heidi Sawyer
ISBN # 978-1-59930-052-8

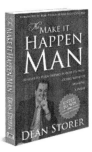

The Make It Happen Man
*10 ways to turn obstacles
into stepping stones without
breaking a sweat*

Dean Storer
ISBN # 978-1-59930-077-1

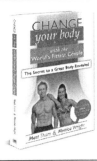

Change your body
Change your life
*with the Fittest Couple in
the World*

Matt Thom &
Monica Wright
ISBN # 978-1-59930-065-8

Good Vibrations!
*Can you tune in to a more
positive life?*

Clare Tonkin
ISBN # 978-1-59930-064-1

The Millionaire Genius
*How to wake up the money
magic within you.*

David Ogunnaike
ISBN # 978-1-59930-026-9

Scoring Eagles
*Improve Your Score In Golf,
Business and Life*

Max Carbone
ISBN # 978-1-59930-045-0

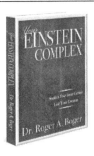

The Einstein Complex
*Awaken your inner genius,
live your dream.*

Dr. Roger A. Boger
ISBN # 978-1-59930-055-9

OTHER BOOKS FROM LIFESUCCESS PUBLISHING

System of Success
*10 Principles of Self
Empowerment to Enhance
Personal Performance*

Stephen and Karen Byrne
ISBN # 978-1-59930-085-6

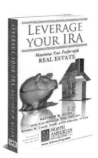

Leverage Your IRA
*Maximize Your Profits with
Real Estate*

Matthew M. Allen
ISBN # 978-1-59930-097-9

The Visionary Leader
*How to inspire success from
the top down*

Susan Bagyura
ISBN # 978-1-59930-094-8

Faith and Fire
*How to Walk Through
Life Without Getting
Burnt*

Roberta Anne Brunin
ISBN # 978-1-59930-090-0

Breakthrough 2 Balance
*Your journey to emotional
freedom*

Alex Reed
ISBN # 978-1-59930-127-3

The Magnetic CEO
*A Handbook for Attracting
and Retaining the Brightest
and the Best*

Dr. Dalia R.E. Lavon
ISBN # 978-1-59930-079-5

Migrating to Australia
A Guidebook

Christine & Erskine Rodan
ISBN # 978-1-59930-067-2

Success Engineering
*The incredible real-life
science behind the Science
of Success, and how to make
it work for you.*

Philip Gosling
ISBN # 978-1-59930-114-3

Printed in the United States
137796LV00003BA/5/P